On Death, Dying and Not Dying

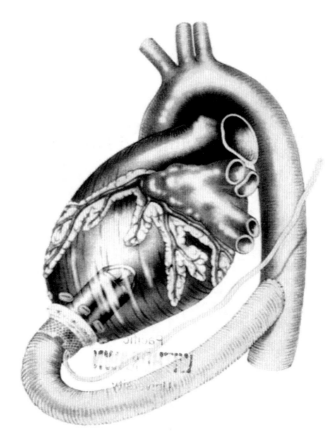

The Jarvik 2000 Heart Pump installed in a human heart
© *Steve Westaby, The Artificial Heart Fund*

On Death,
Dying and Not Dying

Peter Houghton

Jessica Kingsley Publishers
London and Philadelphia

First published in the United Kingdom in 2001 by
Jessica Kingsley Publishers Ltd,
116 Pentonville Road,
London N1 9JB,
England
and
325 Chestnut Street,
Philadelphia, PA 19106, USA.

www.jkp.com

Library of Congress Cataloging in Publication Data
A CIP catalog record for this book is available from the Library of Congress

British Library Cataloguing in Publication Data
A CIP catalogue record for this book is available from the British Library

ISBN 1 84310 020 7

Printed and Bound in Great Britain by
Athenaeum Press, Gateshead, Tyne and Wear

Contents

Preface

In many ways this is a very personal book about the time I was dying and about my earlier work with dying people and their carers. I have tried to be as objective as possible about my own experience and that of others, but I am not sure I have always succeeded. It may be impossible to be so; it was a very obsessing matter, dying.

I am grateful to my friend Rob George for much of the medical information included in the book. Spending time with Rob, one of the leading Palliative Care Consultants, was always an inspiration and sometimes a shock. He taught me a great deal and it was his intervention that gave me access to the clinical trial that saved my life.

I remembered, as I wrote this book, all those people who died whom I had worked with and others, friends and relatives. I am especially grateful to the five people whose stories I have included. I have learned so much from them, and their responses to adversity made me less afraid, more hopeful about my own death.

I may not have said enough about the experience of carers in this book. They are involved in death and are having to cope with it as the dying person moves to a more interior experience and greater physical dependence. My wife, I know, found the whole experience daunting and had to make her own preparations for a life without me. Carers need understanding and support; they have in many respects a thankless task. They need care, knowing the end result will be a loss for them. I respected and supported those who cared for me and for others.

I am grateful to Robert Jarvik who invented the heart pump that gave me renewed life, and to Stephen Westaby and the team of surgeons, doctors and nurses who operated on me and nursed me through the hard times. I was lucky to meet them – and lucky that they dared to experiment.

I am grateful to Steve Westaby and Adrian Banning for their contributions to this book.

I have a friend, Val Gotheridge, who has been my secretary for over 30 years. It is not too much to say that her wish to continue, as she puts it, 'to be useful', helped me write this book; after all I had to have something for her to do!

Thanks too to my long-suffering wife who shared the pain of these times with me with love and understanding.

All this said and properly acknowledged, however, is one side of the coin. The other is the feeling that all is not well with society's attitude to death and our somewhat beleagered health service.

Are we too afraid of death and the messy process of dying? We certainly tend to ignore it except when we have to take account of it. I think we need to be better educated about the process of dying and death itself. It might be as important to include a basic knowledge of death and dying in school curricula as it is knowledge about sexual education. The subject could be taught not of itself but as part of the study of the human body and the stages of human life. Why is this not part of the general curriculum? Why are our bodies made a mystery?

I lay in hospital, had excellent professional care, but the hospital itself seemed to me bucolic. I kept thinking of a painting in Birmingham Art Gallery called *Pandemonium – the Capital of Hell*. Pandemonium seems to me what lies behind the ordered routines of the Ward. Pandemonium about resource scarcity and allocation, pandemonium about staffing and recruitment. The hospital was like a big ship in need of a refit and a new start. I don't think it was any kind of exception.

It is a matter of money, but not wholly so. There is something curiously awry in the way we see hospitals, piecemeal rather than as a whole. I hope the new emphasis on quality control will improve this, but somehow it seems to me it may not; rather it will add to the pandemonium – yet another thing to be coped with. Some radical thinking about how we provide health care seems to me to be needed.

I hope good palliation will be available as a matter of course for the dying and that the procedure used to help me will become as commonplace as bypass surgery; that alone would make my experience worthwhile.

Peter Houghton
June 2001

Chapter 1
My Own Story

It is hard to know where to start this story — we are the products of our own history and the onset of heart disease was just one factor in my life. It came to be the determining factor, likely to end my life. Looking back now at the little miracle I have experienced and want to tell you about, means I have to say why I feel able to say anything at all about death and dying.

This is not any kind of autobiography; it is about 'Not Dying', so I do not want to set out or summarize my life. I think I have had a vivid, unusual life, and an unusually strong acquaintance with death throughout it. An acquaintance that has been both personal in terms of family loss and professional in that I have been someone who counseled dying people and their relatives. Counseling also reveals other kinds of death just as it does the many varieties of griefs. Circumstances change, relationships end, children become adults; in a way they are all little deaths evoking from us elements of grief and uncertainty about the future.

I retain in my mind the images and memories of those people who have passed on whom I loved and also those people who died as I worked with them, who showed me what it is to be human.

I was born and brought up in the Midlands, mostly in Birmingham, except for some years in South Africa because of a family connection. Those years in South Africa were very influential in my life and it was there I began my acquaintance with death. In the end, however, I am a 'Brummie' and I guess that is where my roots are.

I am married but we have no children. This has been one of the deep regrets of my life. I, even now, feel jealous when I see what medical advances have made possible for the infertile these days and wish they had been available for us. That is one of the griefs I carry. In 1976 I set going The National Association for the Childless, now the National Fertility Society, to work for improved chances of treatment for couples struggling to conceive. It is a work that has endured beyond me and so I conclude it must have been valuable.

I had the chance in the early seventies to do two other things of which I am proud. The first was to develop the first Money Advice Centre at Birmingham Settlement where I was Director. This provided debt counseling for the hugely increased number of people with debt problems. I got the first local authority grant for such a project from the now defunct West Midlands County Council. Again, these services have expanded and had a life beyond me and I am proud I began the process.

One of the things I did with long-term consequences in my life was care for adolescents who had problems of various kinds. I did that at Birmingham Settlement in the early seventies. Some had no families of their own, others faced family breakdown and rejection, and others struggled with personal problems that made it impossible for their parents to cope with them. Some of the relationships forged in that period with those young people have endured and been valuable to me as sources of encouragement and support and, of course, of grief and pain! During my ill health many of the people from those times showed me real love and concern.

I suppose, in terms of this book, my work as a counselor to dying people is what counts most; yet to me it is just one of the things I did in a long forty years' working life. What makes it important is that as I did this work I became terminally ill myself and so was able to compare what I was feeling with those of the people I had advised.

This story of my imminent death and almost miracu-
lous resurrection thus begins with a weight of personal
history behind it. I hope you will keep in mind something of who I am as you read it. I am not just a person
who nearly died.

According to my own doctors in early June 2000 I
was weeks not months away from death. 'I'd give you
three to four weeks', one of them told me. It was no surprise, I could feel my symptoms worsening and knew
that without some drastic intervention I would die soon.
It was both a frightening and a relieving prospect. There
are attractions in the idea it could soon be all over, as
well as fear of the process itself and the unknown.

I lived in denial of my coming death. I knew it was
near, was aware of what I had come to call the sense of
bodily dissolution I felt physically. I was able to prepare
such things as leaving an idea of what I wanted at my
funeral, saying goodbye to friends. I knew death was a
process, had seen that process many times, thought
about it as such, but I only vaguely experienced it in that
way. Death was something not arrived: I might go on
longer than people thought, and I couldn't spend each
day wondering how I was deteriorating. Thus alongside
the awareness of death coming was a denial that it was
as near or imminent as it was.

I was also aware of psychological changes. These included an increase in my acceptance and reliance upon

my Catholicism in contrast to my earlier more agnostic view of Catholicism and religion in general. I wondered if this was a fear reaction, I cannot be sure but I don't think it was only that. Extremity focused me on something profound within. It was my own real experience of God. This was sustaining in my crisis of life, but trying to analyse precisely how defeats me. It just was.

Another psychological effect was a sense of 'no matter'. For example, I needed some new shoes, but felt it pointless to buy them because of the effort in going to do so and the likelihood I would hardly wear them. This is a trivial incident in itself, but was very much part of my general feeling. I decided to end my life by writing a personal testament of God based on my experiences. I called it *The Nine Descents of the Spirit.* I had to force myself to finish it, doubting whether it would be useful, ever read, or whether it had had anything original in it. I was relieved when it was done – that was that, I was ready to go. There was, however, also something life affirming about writing that. It was a kind of refusal as Dylan Thomas observed, to go quietly 'into that good night'.

Anguish

Being better, you forget how bad you were. I wrote to my friend Liz in America on 10th March 2000; this extract explains my anguish and sickness as I felt it then.

'What am I doing with myself. Not much, read the paper, had a shower, did some ironing – exhausted. Fancied an orange, ate one, puked, exhausted again. Doctor comes, says I am a bit better!! Yelled at her. She ups the dose of antibiotics, the kidney infection is back in a big way, she says, we must really zap it. We? She points out I have solved the sleeping problem. True, one hour's sleep, get up and puke etc – whole night like this. She says this is better than staying awake between the bouts. She goes, will come again tomorrow to monitor me. Am turning into a lizard I think.

Go through the mail, throw most of it away. Try the E Mail – can't be bothered and puke. Have I become a malfunctioning organism where what usually is used to fuel it, is now used to re-gurgitate. Milkman comes for his money, pay him; he mentions how I am losing weight and look a bit pale. Do not puke on him – exercise restraint. He tells me how his aunt's husband's best friend had something similar to what I have got, not that he knows what it is and found drinking hot black currant juice helpful. I thank him for his undoubted insight. Everybody knows someone who has been miraculously helped by something, even if they are now dead.

Almine phones me from Canada where she says the vibes of the universe told her I was needy today. She offers to say an Atlantean prayer with me; decline to do this. She says I will, as everyone does, choose the time of my death, it is up to me, she will see if she can get some energy in my chakras. Thanked her and think to myself, bananas.

16

Diane rings to find how I am doing — I say naff, she says, so is she today.

Ahmad tells me to hang in there; tell him I want out of here. Terry tells me to hang in there too — splutter. Malcolm comes and goes out to do some errands for me. He says I am dying, so he better be nice to me — bastard!

Clare next door tells me, as I lean out of the window getting some air, that I look better than I have done. I can see she is being nice.'

What got me to this experience of dying and then drew me back from the brink of death?

Cardiomyopathy

One evening in March 1996 I had what amounted to a mild heart attack. It was just after a bad bout of influenza and later the doctor felt that might have triggered the heart attack. I am not sure; I had been increasingly breathless for a year or two and begun to have edema. In any event this incident revealed I had a cardiomyopathy with a consequent leaking mitral valve. An operation to improve the valve was considered but rejected on the grounds that in improving the valve, the pressure resulting on the damaged heart wall would lead inevitably to another probably fatal heart attack. It was decided to help my heart with drugs that improved its function in various ways. These were beta blockers, ace inhibitors, digoxin, warfarin. This did seem to control my condition for a time although I never felt well again after that heart event.

A doctor friend of mine, experienced in palliative care, explained to me fully what I might expect. She told me that the drugs would inhibit but not stop the worsening of my condition; very slowly, imperceptibly sometimes, things would get worse, the drugs would require larger dosage to be effective and eventually would not be able to cope. This proved to be an accurate prediction of what actually happened. By October 1999 my condition had measurably worsened and from that time other symptoms multiplied. By February 2000 I was told my heart was able to pump only ten per cent of the blood I needed through the arteries, there was now some damage to the right heart and basically I was clinging on. It was decided the time had come to assess me for a transplant, the only possible chance of reversing the progress of my heart failure. However by June I had still not had an appointment for this assessment, was notably worse and realizing I would never live long enough to benefit from a transplant.

Apart from increased breathlessness, the worst symptoms were itching, gout, weight gain from edema, fungal sores on my skin all over my body, dry and dead skin on my legs and feet, sleeplessness and appetite loss. I knew my kidneys were going to fail, just hoped they wouldn't. I prepared for death: this is the inevitable result of a cardiomyopathy.

Preparing for death

It is not easy to prepare for death. It involves a change of attitude that some of my psychological feelings earlier described symptomized. Letting go of relationships and ambitions in life was hard to do, but as you did it the significance of the affairs of life diminished. Life began to seem more like a dream from which I was awakening. I used to smile inwardly when, while vomiting, which I did often, my wife would come in all concerned to see what she could do, which was not much except offer moral support. I said to myself, 'Doesn't she realize things will be better for her when all this is over?'. And, of course, she did know that I did not credit enough her sense of love. In the vastness of things, in the span of our lives, the history of the universe, my vomiting near the end of my life was trivial, unimportant, however unpleasant it might be. Nothing made life seem more diminished than the leaving of it.

I always, in appropriate cases, advocated that dying people should try to do last things. That is, wind up their lives, finish unfinished business, make amends or apologise where necessary, and say thank you. So when I realized I was going to die I decided to take my own advice.

It was comparatively easy to wind up my life. My wife would look after my affairs and, indeed, largely took them over. I said goodbye to my friends and the young people we had known by planning my funeral. I asked them to come, to carry the coffin, narrate one of my poems and so on. They were all happy to do it, but their reactions varied. Interestingly only one tried to say I was being too pessimistic, it wouldn't happen. The rest were happy to talk about the good times in our relationships and to agree to this last task. This was more disconcerting than I thought it would be. This was not because they accepted the fact I was near death, but because talking about our relationships in this way illustrated that they were in the past. So really it told me it was over, no need to worry, that was that.

This insight was fine when I was dying, it enabled me to feel my life was complete and had been appreciated. It proved more difficult when I survived as we shall see.

Apologizing was good too. I do not want to dwell here on the things in my life I had not been proud of, they remain painful memories and forgiving myself for them is incomplete. Apologizing, however, was a surprise, some felt things were in the past and had passed by. They were no longer alive to them as they were to me. Others thanked me and pointed out it was myself I harmed more than them. Still others felt there was

nothing to forgive and never had been. It was confusing. Had I lived too long with the pain of bad things
when they had really passed away? It gave me a new
perspective. These things were over, were part of my
life, made me more human, and they had not led to
hatred as I thought but to renewal, even if I was the salu-
tary lesson for that renewal. For the first time I felt able
to accept myself, my life and not to worry about the
darkness in it.

Saying thank you was also good, it led to much
remembering of good things and then of their consequences in peoples lives. I realized I had done some
good, had been useful, could die knowing that my life
had, within its small context, meant something, changed
something. I also realized people needed to be thanked,
that by thanking I was being just and true to our
sharing. It made me feel less isolated, I could leave in the
knowledge the good had outweighed the bad.

This process took a little time, I began it in February
2000 and it ended only in mid May when I became too
ill. I was fortunate I had more or less finished what I felt
I needed to do. It was a relief, but it was also much more
stark than I had anticipated. All you had to do now was
face your own death and the dying process. You had in
effect left the world before you died. It was quite frightening to be confronted only with managing your own
deterioration. In the day things happened, you could

keep a bit occupied even if it was only the nurse calling, or the occupational therapist with some new equipment. At night, there was suffering, as you had to deal with your symptoms, desperate to sleep you were sick, and there was that underlying fear that the end would come. It is hard to explain how much we want to choose life over death biologically. We cannot, I think, actually imagine our death. Maybe that is a mercy for otherwise we would know too much. There are, of course, things to imagine, to hope for, like an after life, but the actual moment of death must always be a surprise, it isn't happening to us. As the time grew closer I longed for the rest and hopefully new life death would bring, but I did not, for one moment, see my death, it was beyond my imagination.

And then something happened.

Deciding to have a go at living a bit longer

A doctor friend of mine, concerned about my condition and knowing as a palliative care specialist I was near death, went to see a cardiologist colleague to see what more might be done to relieve my symptoms, especially the gout which was intensely painful. While waiting to see him he read a notice in which a Consultant at the John Radcliffe Hospital, Oxford, announced a clinical trial of the Jarvik Heart Assist Device and that he was looking for suitable patients to join the trial. He phoned up and twenty-four hours later I was sitting in Steve Westaby's office in Oxford having this new radical and largely untried approach to the treatment of cardiomyopathy explained to me.

It all seemed overwhelming and difficult, even though they were enthusiastic to do it and confident the Jarvik pump once installed could give me a new life. Their enthusiasm appealed to my remaining wish to live and so I agreed to allow them to medically assess my suitability for the procedure. I did not really expect to be well enough to undergo such a major piece of surgery in my poor physical condition. I was a bit surprised, therefore, after some tests when they said I could, but that as I was very near a point of no return it had to be done quickly. This meant I had to make a decision whether to try it or at least let my name go forward to the people who supervised clinical trials. I had to think about this when it came down to it. On the one hand to grab a chance of life however remote seemed worth it, on the other might it not be best to let myself die now as I was reluctantly prepared to do? Who knew what suffering or likelihood of success there was from such a treatment as a bridge to recovery.

I knew that the Jarvik pump had been used before as a bridge to transplant, or for a temporary reason, so I knew the pump could be successfully installed. How long it might last, or what the quality of life might be subsequently was hard to ascertain. It would be good to know whether the authorities agreed with the Radcliffe team's recommendation that I should have the operation. I did not realize that a large part of that assessment was to decide whether I really did assent to the offer and had not been persuaded against my instincts by the team's enthusiasm; my own will to recover was also important in this. So I had to make the decision instinctively despite the uncertainties.

I think it was the shock of learning I was less than a month from death that finally influenced me. I had expected to have the time to go to my wife's 60th birthday celebration in mid September and to see the birth of a first child to one of the youngsters who had lived with us and whom we had cared for. I was trying to live for these little goals and then I thought I could let go. The fact that I could not make it without help to either event was important to me. I thought if the treatment held out the hope of just getting to those goals it was worth trying. This seemed to satisfy the authorities, as it was a realistic assessment of my chances, and provided an understandable goal to live for.

Talking with my wife about it, I was aware of her hesitancy over whether I was doing the right thing. She could barely believe I was so near death, and it was a shock for her to have to deal with the prospect that I might die in the next few days in the operating theatre or in post-operative recovery. She felt, however, it had to be my decision. I realized too she had begun to prepare herself for my death and for her own life afterwards and that she might find it hard to give up those plans.

Once decided I hated the waiting while the preparations were made. I wanted to get it over with. I half listened to what they told me to expect afterwards. I wish now I had listened more carefully because I was most concerned with surviving the procedure and gave too little thought to preparing myself for the trials of the recovery period.

While waiting I had a kind of vision which I inadequately described in poetic form and attach hereto as it shows the mixture of hope and despair I felt.

After the Retreat of Darkness

Cloud covers the Eastern plains,
Pink in the morning light,
I am high on the mountain of deliverance

Last night I looked back at the twinkling cities of the
*   plain*
From where to this long climb I came
'Goodbye', I whispered to the past

And I rested in the shelter of a rowan tree
From which I cut a staff to be
My last taking from the eastern world

And breathless I climbed towards the pass
And I heard God say to me in my heart
Welcome my son

I looked around astonished
But there was only the whisper of the soft wind
And a clear translucent sky

And a fresh stream crossed the path unbridged
Plunging back to the eastern world
I looked eastward, but there I can no longer go

A sleep came on me and I was carried away
Amid dreams and half remembered moments
Among the crags above, bright at noon day

26

And the angel of death who was waiting sang
Do not hold my hand but first speak
To the Keeper of the Gate of Everything

And looking upwards I saw a great light
Where water poured forth and the winds began
'Thou Art' The Keeper said in my head

And I looked down to the west where in beauty
Were the untouched places of the future
With the sea in the far distance

'These Edens' The Keeper said in my head
'Are for you as long as you are That Thou Art'
And I said 'Yes' with all thankfulness of heart

And I woke from my dream and looked down on Eden
And my broken rowan staff was alive
With all the power of making

The operation and the first days after

I remember nothing of the operation. Steve Westaby describes it in the contribution he kindly wrote for this book. I remember being in the foyer of the theatre receiving the anaesthetic and saying the Lord's prayer and a Hail Mary as I sank into sleeping. Somewhere in the time I began to dream vividly and then begin to be aware of my surroundings, surrounded by machines, monitoring equipment and nurses and unable to speak because of intubation. I stayed that way a few days in and out of dream; only slowly did the Recovery Unit become more real than my dreams.

Then one day the tube from my mouth was suddenly gone. I could talk. The team were gathered at the bedside. 'How do you feel?' Steve Westaby asked. I looked at them with affection, I was still there, 'You bloody bastards', I replied. They understood that this was a thank you.

Those days in intensive care are a bit of a blur. Gradually I learned to distinguish my surroundings from the vivid and continuous dream state I experienced. In grasping for a sense of reality, I envisaged myself as sort of being encased in a lozenge which was fed by all sorts of tubes. In a way this was how it was, so I was seeing in metaphorical terms my situation. I liked the lozenge, it seemed safe, painless and cosy. When reality intruded it was usually painful and exhausting, but reality intruded more as time went by. My lozenge time ended one day when they were moving me in the bed, encouraging me to use my legs to help the process. I looked down, surprised at the concept of legs and saw them, felt they were mine and I might use them. 'I am oblong after all', I thought, 'My body still exists'.

Eventually I was disconnected from all the machines, the drips were removed, I became a bit autonomous and was moved out of the Cardiac Recovery Unit (intensive care) to the Cardiothoracic Ward. I felt so glad to be out of the unit, but the worst of the recovery time was only just beginning.

Second stage recovery

The first period of recovery in intensive care, as I look back on it, was the easiest. I dreamt, was not in much pain, slept a lot and was pleased when I could do little things, like getting out of bed by myself. Once I could walk and move, intubation and other items were withdrawn and I could go to the Recovery Ward it was not so easy. This was when the worst experiences I had began. It is hard to pinpoint what were the worst things. Pain was one: not continuous pain, but sharp when I moved and lasting twenty to thirty minutes after I did. Exhaustion was another; everything tired me out. The constant routines of the hospital intruded on my peace. My catheter became very uncomfortable and they removed it – with reluctance, I felt. Then there was a problem with the wire buried in my scalp and neck; it became exposed and I had to undergo its reburial by a plastic surgeon under a local anaesthetic. It was not particularly painful, but it was upsetting just as I felt I had begun to get better. In some ways this need to go back to the operating room diminished my belief in recovery. I became more and more sensitive, less tolerant, both of the care I was receiving and other difficulties of recovery. Nevertheless time went by and slowly I improved. The next dramatic signs of my recovery were progressive weight loss as my system responded to the new blood supply by expelling the edema (I lost over 25 kilos), and the re-supply of blood to my feet, which caused bleeding through the dry skin. I was told also my right heart was healing itself.

The team felt it was time for me to move into a nearby flat as a bridge to rehabilitation. I was reluctant to accept this as exhaustion, pain, and difficulty moving made me wonder if I could manage. Nevertheless I was moved; it was not a success.

Third stage recovery – the flat

It is difficult to explain the relief of being out of the hospital routines and in the flat, or the contrasting fear that my pain and other symptoms would be neglected, and I was not up to even a measure of independence. I know the high costs of care paid, as they were, by a charity may have necessitated early departure from the Ward, but looking back on it, I was not ready but could not convince them of this.

The time in the flat is a blur. Severe constipation resulting from pain-killing drugs added both to the pain and general discomfort. I was not really well enough to entertain myself through reading or going for walks. The staff took me on country drives, which were great, but exquisitely painful; one took me out to dinner, but I had poor appetite. In the end I felt myself deteriorating. I caught an infection, had a raised temperature and had to go back to the Ward. I didn't want to go but was deeply relieved when I did; maybe now someone would notice the pain I was in and believe me.

Fourth stage recovery

Back in the ward I struggled for a time. The infection improved, but I had severe bouts of gout which made me almost immobile. One of my minor wounds in my groin began to leak copiously a sort of colourless fluid, but nevertheless with a nasty smell. They had to open it up in another operation to drain out the infection. This was also done under local anaesthetic and by this time I had had enough, so was more sensitive to the pain. They also took the opportunity to remove a large lipoma.

This wound took a very long time to heal, it wept, bled and had to be restitched twice. It was painful as the tight stitching pulled against the flesh. Changing the dressings was unpleasant as the sticky tape had to be pulled off, and all the time the pain continued in my upper abdomen.

The consultant was certain the pain was from the healing of the thoracotomy wound. I am sure that was a factor, but as this pain still recurs from time to time, notably when my stomach is full, I have come to think that the basic cause is the pressure on the heart pump from an inflated stomach. It is the only time I am conscious the pump is there.

Recovery was a long slow process on the Ward, but eventually they and I felt it was possible for me to go home and recuperate further there. By this time the infected wound was at last healing and the worst of the pain was over. I was still exhausted, without appetite and nervous.

At home

It was a great relief to be at home; after ten-and-a-half weeks the hospital routines had begun to make me feel institutionalized; I still call the place Colditz to this day. Yet it was not all progress at home. I had another infection and was in hospital for ten days again, but once the stitches from the groin wound were removed, the pain eased, it became easier to walk and it was great to be able to go for a walk again after many years. The team keep a close eye on me, but care is now more with my GP. The GP practice were very good; they took the trouble to learn about the procedure and came to see me regularly, as did the nurses based in the practice. I felt supported in my recovery, both by the Oxford team and the General Practice; no little problem was too much – I felt safe and wanted. The Practice was even able to arrange for me to see a psychologist to talk over, as I needed to, this strange situation which felt a bit like a resurrection. I felt like Lazarus!

Nowadays I can walk longish distances (three to five miles), feel generally well and am less exhausted. Further progress may be unlikely; it is hard to say. Certainly it is much slower if it is occurring at all. I am coming to accept the irritating attachment to a battery and periodic discomfort when my stomach is full. I am not sure I will ever feel robustly healthy again, but I can cope and do have some quality of life for now; it is a chance in a million.

Was it worth it?

Some days, coping with an infection or pain, I think possibly not! You look forward and see more of the same to be endured indefinitely. As I am not much afraid of death as an alternative, it does not look so bad. I even worry if my pump lasts a hundred years, will I be able to die! I expect other things will fail before it might.

Living with uncertainty is also different. What will I be strong enough to do, how far can I travel given the need to plug and recharge several times a day; no-one knows how long the pump will last. I have had one inside longer than anyone else, although when I looked at the one removed from a man on transplant, who had worn it for seven months, it seemed clear, undamaged and functionally unimpaired.

The Birmingham cardiothoracic surgeon offered me the possibility of going for a transplant, knowing the pumps were mostly used as a bridge to it. It was a tempting offer, but it seemed to me I could do more good by keeping it, seeing to what extent it could be a 'bridge to recovery', thus obviating a part of the need for many transplants. Also the idea of another major operation appalled me. I have had my chance, let others take the opportunity offered by transplants.

Of course I am deeply grateful for the privilege of participating in the trial, and have much love and respect for the team who gave me life. It is given to few people to be so aided and so surrounded with affection. That too is unforgettable as an experience and was a real aid to my recovery.

Returning to life

I seem to have experienced re-entering the living world in three stages. I call them the exhibit stage, the confused stage, and the re-emergence. They are not clearly defined and overlap into each other, but they have distinctive characteristics.

I have wondered why I see it in stages; I think it is partly to do with the state of health or recovery, partly to do with a reluctance to return to old things in any way, partly because you are afraid how those around you will react and partly because you are actually somewhat different as a result of the experience. I have not been able to recover the intensity of my involvement with life, it seems more whimsical, I feel more an observer than a participant. It is not that I lack ambitions for the future, or a wish to be useful, just that it doesn't matter so much. I have been collecting little experiences, nothing unusual about them, but they seem curiously vivid, as if life's new savour is not concerned with the big things, but the day to day. Let me tell you what I mean with a couple of examples.

I am sitting in the waiting room at the Dental Hospital. I am having to go because during my operation they managed to loosen or dislodge all my crowns and one or two fillings. The room is one of those nondescript places of passage, the seats are a bit low and worn, everyone is a bit self-absorbed. I have had an antibiotic and am having to wait for it to work before being tortured! When in comes a young man. He is enormous, I am not thin, but he immediately makes me feel waifish. He sort of stands there unhappily, aware I think, of the O my God stares of the people waiting. He is so large he is sweating profusely and bursting out of his clothes. One fears he might break one of the chairs if he sat on one, or that he will expire from breathlessness if he does not. He is also eating a large bag of crisps with a dedication rarely seen.

I wonder what is wrong with him, so I smile and say 'come to be tortured' while shifting so he can sit next to me. He looks surprised. He sits down, 'got a bad tooth-ache?' I ask. 'I have' he says in quite a posh accent. I notice he smells sweaty. 'You must find things very diffi-cult with all that weight' I say to him. He looks at me. 'In five years, you are the first stranger ever to be honest about it. I've got a syndrome, don't burn enough energy, always want to eat.' I can see that from the way he is de-vouring the crisps. I want to take his crisps off him, but well, it might cause a scene. 'Can't anything be done to help you?', I ask. 'I take more pills and have seen more doctors than you will ever know' he replies, 'and am in for a short life'. This is a bit troubling so I tell him how very good they are at the dental hospital and how, if ever I got to be a God, an unlikely event, I would reinvent teeth. At this a diminutive dental nurse comes and takes him into the inner sanctum. I see him once more, half upside down with a dentist drilling merrily in his mouth.

I thought to myself, this is a young man, not above thirty, he has a Mom and Dad somewhere who have few hopes of him, he faces an early death, and must experi-ence every day almost total isolation as he looks repul-sive. *Kyrie eleison*, I think, *Kyrie eleison, Christe eleison*.

I am in the Albert Hall watching a performance of *Aida*. The lead tenor invited me as he polished my heart pump. This in itself is odd, that a tenor should polish heart pumps, even more as he is Chinese and lives in New York. Apparently the man who invented the heart pump is an opera fan and kind of took responsibility for the Chinese tenor, when his visa ran out and he needed to earn money for his training in order to stay in the States. So he became a pump polisher.

I am not very keen on *Aida*, it is a rather grim opera with the hero and heroine ending up entombed. Robert Jarvik and his wife are there and also another lady to whose flat in the Albert Mansions we go for drinks after the glum ending of the opera. You need a drink to cheer you up, as my aunt Violet would say in the pub after going to mass. The lady turned out to be Persian, and not just that, but a descendant of the last Qajar Shah. Her flat is an artist's paradise of both Persian antiquities and other art. She is surprised I know a bit about Persian art and poetry and we discuss the merits of various Persian poets a while, she likes Hafiz, I prefer Rumi.

Is this strange, I think, pump polishers and Persian Shah descendents, life is very rich – essentially this was trivial, but I was glad of the zest of the triviality.

My point is, that I am experiencing something, but I am detached, uninvolved. I still feel only half here.

The Exhibit

In those times I lay in bed, wandered painfully around the Ward, or came home feeling exhausted – I couldn't do much. I read quite a bit, chatted to the other patients, got to know the staff, enjoyed visitors, ate reluctantly, drank insufficiently and generally felt lethargic. Almost from the first I got visited, by people interested in the new procedure, by friends wanting to see how I was doing. I was not passive, I tried to play my part, did not want to upset anyone. I felt like an exhibit.

It was quite good being an exhibit, something I could do. I could tell that people were pleased with my progress and wanted to show me off. Sometimes the visits were official, surgeons and doctors from overseas for example, including a veritable delegation from Japan on one occasion. Nurses from other wards would pop in to have a look; always if I felt well enough, the visitors from the local Catholic church took it in turns to visit me so they could see what had been done, and I guess to a Catholic too! All this was extra to the routines of after-care, physiotherapists, people who brought the food around and then the tea, nurses checking on you and often wanting a chat. On one memorable day, when those Japanese came, I counted no less than twenty-seven people came to see me in one way or another. It was like living in the Tate Modern.

I basked in the fame and attention, was glad to be useful. It was about all I could do at the time. I felt being an exhibit was not so bad, but then, it began to get boring and intrusive. When yet another person wanted to see my head plug, as I call it, cranial pedestal as they do, I felt like saying my head was not for viewing except by appointment. But by this time the press had got the story and I was even more of an exhibit. Not a lot of people have had their innards pictured in the Sunday Times colour supplement! My whole life became of interest; this was difficult, as I am a bit private. My wife and family got angry with me because of the intrusion into their lives. It was overwhelming. And yet I wanted to tell my story – something drives me to do so. I am still struggling with the instinct to privacy and the need to talk about my experience and life to this day. Celebrity status, be it involuntary, has been a very mixed blessing.

I think it was the burgeoning press interest that moved me on from just being a kind of passive exhibit to wanting to do something again, but what?

Confusion

As I began to feel I might be able to take charge of some kind of life again I began to ask questions. The results were confusing. The main questions were, what am I well enough to do and likely to be able to do, what do I want to do, and who am I now.

I think it is still not clear what I might be well enough to do. No-one has ever had a heart pump in as a permanent treatment before, or ever as long as I have, so that what will happen is largely therefore informed extrapolation or guesswork. How long will the pump last...don't know, it should last indefinitely. Is my heart recovering still...yes but not so fast now, seems to have reached a plateau. We don't know how it will develop. Am I a disabled person, after all I get the allowance...yes you are, but not entirely. So it is up to me to decide what I can and cannot do.

I guess you have to feel within to see how you are. That is disconcerting because it is clear to me, from all the little signs of daily performance, that I would die but for the pump. Physically I am a lot stronger, feel renewed, but underlying it the sense of death remains. This is extra time. I have no idea how long this time will last, it is like being on the Titanic.

Given that I am clearly disabled and a bit dead, what do I want to do with this time? I want something new, something I can be proud to do, something different. In a way my walks in aid of the Artificial Heart Fund and the National Heart Research Fund are tests. Whatever money I can raise is needed to help other patients, but for me, it is to see how strong I am, to repay what I owe at least in part. If I can make it, then I guess I will be

strong enough to travel, to do most things. Yet in prac-
tising along the canals, I realise I am a bit unwell still.

Writing this book, getting it all off my chest, has
been a part of my purpose recently; it seemed the right
thing to do. I like writing and I can sit at a computer, no
problems. However it is a finite task, the book; what will
come after? Will anyone want me to write anything
else? Have I got anything worth saying? I wish someone
would take an interest in my science fiction writing, but
I get only rejections!

I don't want to return to work. I never want to advise
or counsel another person about dying. I don't quite
know why; I think it was because of having seen things
from the perspective of the counseled. I needed counseling and was fortunate to be referred to someone excellent who did her very best to understand how I was
feeling and help me come to terms with it. I realized
how important the counselor was, how they had to
understand enough but not to pretend to understand all.
All the things I had been taught, and suddenly I did not
want to ever do it again. If there were people as good as
the counselor I was seeing, why did I need to do it? It
made me feel free to decide this. For the first time I felt
retired by my own choice. It was a good feeling, but I
still had no idea what I wanted to do.

I think the most confusing thing was in my relationships. I felt, and continue to feel, they were all in the

past. It is not that I don't have any, or am not happily returned to my wife, on the contrary, things are better than they have been. It is just that I have seen that she and the others can have a life without me, that it would be fine for them and so I feel it might be the same for me. I am not actually needed any more. I have done my bit, played the part I was due to play in their lives and they in mine. I love their friendship and support, need it now and then, but they are the past I said goodbye to when I was dying. I want to find the relationships or develop new ones with them that will have passion for me in the future. I hope I can find a new mutuality with some of my old friends, my wife and family, but I have not found it yet.

And then one day, sitting in rare spring sunshine on a bench in a rose garden, I remembered a piece from a poem by T.S. Eliot. I am not quoting it correctly, just as I recalled it – 'Because I do not hope, Because I do not hope to turn, Desiring this man's gifts or that man's wealth. Because I do not hope'. It becomes necessary to create something upon which to hope. Now how do I do that, I felt with a sudden surge of hope in my heart.

Re-emergence

It is difficult to write about a process incomplete, not yet defined, but that is like life I guess. It is never tidy, rarely clear, and always assailed by doubt. Indeed doubt seems to be almost a way of life these days.

I guess that moment in the rose garden began a quest. It is good being on a quest, a pilgrim. Everything is new, you are looking for something, something you will only know when you find it and then, probably, you will be disappointed in it and move on. What I am trying to do is sort things out so that the quest may be the central task of my life.

Three things matter. First having enough cash to do what I might want to do. So I better earn a bit and supplement my annuity and my disablement allowance. You don't earn much from book authorship these days, if you ever did. I am no Jeffrey Archer thank heavens! So my task is to finish it, after all it is an obligation, and then do something that brings in some cash. I am still thinking through some ideas, but it will come to me.

And this minor celebrity stuff. Well if you can't beat it you might as well enjoy it. I am trying to do that and to sell the book in so doing! It isn't easy to enjoy it though; my wife resolutely hates it, but I am learning, slowly, what makes a good story. I hope though it will be more than just enjoying it. I hope I can do something for the many people suffering from cardiomyopathy and can say something to people about the experience of dying that helps their own when it comes.

I decided as I liked writing science fiction I was going to make a job of it and I have begun to do that, creating an alternative future and form for the human race. It is fun to do, I just hope, one day, someone will think it might be fun to publish or make a TV thing of. Anyway I will have a go, I might become the Rodenberry of the zeros. If anyone wants to know what I think the universe of the 31st century will be like, write to me!

I am sure that something I must do would be what I call wise creating. I know about Settlements as I spent nearly twenty years running one. It was good fun, you could be innovative in the social interest. I admire the people who founded Settlements, not so much for their motives though they were for the most part laudable, but because they established institutions that have survived the tests of time and change, not without loss, but they remain at the radical edge of social experiment. Of course I do not want to run a Settlement again, but it would be good to make a contribution to founding some institution that would last a hundred years, so I am looking.

I shall try and found a new organization for those having extra life because of medical intervention in a mechanical way. Maybe that will lead to something.

Re-emergence involves having dreams; they may be unrealistic, but they have to be there. Life is about dreaming new dreams and then deciding what it is possible to do with them. I hope I dream some fine new dreams.

Very slowly I am getting the energy to have some kind of life for myself. It isn't easy, but I feel hopeful of those other Edens I saw in my mind's eye just before the operation. Now it seems more like this:

I came to think the western light o'er seaward lands
Elusive like the singing sands,
Was a distant prospect beckoning
Within death's own reckoning.

But slowly down the vale I tread
Sometimes with hope, sometimes with dread
And the blissful light grows nearer
And life's new lease feels ever dearer.

Chapter 2

The Physical
Process of Dying

What was physically happening to me and the people I tried to help when they were dying? How do we die? In this chapter I am going to set out the process of dying. I am indebted to my friend and former colleague Rob George, Consultant in Palliative Medicine at University College Hospital, London whose concepts I have used to explain the process.

The first thing to understand is that, except in the case of accidents or a fatal heart attack, death is a process rather than a single event. We die over a period of time though at various rates of progress according to the illness and our own general condition. While we may be terminally ill at the beginning of the process we are not usually in the terminal stage of the process, so we need to anticipate and have some understanding of what is ahead. How long will it be, for example, until I am bed ridden and unable to do things for myself? Will the pain be bad and how will it be controlled? When we realize we are terminally ill we want to have some idea of how long we have got and some reassurance our symptoms will be controlled.

The problem is that everything depends on something else so it is very difficult to be precise about either matter although pain can be and is generally well controlled. I found it helpful to understand what is ahead of me as a process with more or less distinct stages and to be able to assess what stage I was in.

If we are a carer, friend of the dying person or family member we must remember that we will have a fraught encounter with the dying person. It will distress us, involve us, take our time and draw perhaps unwonted attention to fundamental things in our own lives and our own health. The assumption we all make is that death is a bad thing, a negative circumstance, but really it is a simple fact of life, understandable like any other such as childbirth. So in this chapter I am trying to be rational, even neutral about death. My aim is to show what we encounter and why and what can be done to help.

Palliative care

I think we need to make a distinction between palliative care and other forms of care, curative in intent. In palliative care the aim is not to prevent the progress of an illness but to relieve its symptoms so the sufferer can die as pain free and with as much dignity as possible. The word 'palliate' derives from the Latin *palliare* (to cloak). This is exactly what palliative medicine does; it cloaks the symptoms of the illness as far as possible. There can be many symptoms, pain, nausea and vomiting, breathlessness, inanition[1], anxiety and physical agitation. Lesser problems also arise in many cases such as skin ulceration, pressure sores, weight loss, mouth sores etc. All these need to be controlled and the patient relieved as a result. The aim is to ensure the patient is not agonized with pain, vomiting, breathlessness or anxiety and restlessness and that any symptoms of nausea or diarrhea are controlled.

Palliative care usually begins alongside curative treatment, but in the end is the main relief for the sufferer. Palliation can, by reducing symptoms; cause periods of relative stability and a slowing down of the dying process because of the sufferer's improved morale and well being. What actually happens is that the condition plateaus for a time and this does enable the sufferer

---

1   There is a glossary of medical terms at the back of the book.

to have a better quality of life, which, if their symptoms were badly controlled, would not be possible. Palliation by its very nature, however, is not curative.

Stages

One way of understanding the dying process that one day we will all face is by seeing it as a series of stages. These merge into each other and vary in length according to circumstances, but they were part of my experience as a dying person and I saw these stages in others.

1. A potentially fatal illness has been diagnosed and available treatments are being applied, plus any pain or other relief needed. The sufferer and his or her family may or may not know of the possible terminal consequences if treatment fails. The emphasis is on cure and defeat of the condition.

2. Treatment has failed or is no longer able to arrest the progress of the disease significantly. The side effects of treatment may be exceeding its benefit. Treatment is withdrawn either gradually or abruptly and medical care concentrates on symptom control, particularly pain relief. Attempts are made to cope with emotional distress and to prepare for death or resist it with dignity.

3. The disease has progressed so the sufferer needs constant care and attention. The number of symptoms multiply as the general condition of the body deteriorates and growing physical weakness and wasting makes them dependent on others.

In the first stage the sufferer maintains a reasonable level of independence and has hope of a successful outcome notwithstanding periodic depression. The second stage is more difficult as the sufferer must come to terms with the imminent prospect of death and will most likely slowly accumulate further symptoms showing increasing bodily weakness as time passes. The third stage means that death itself is relatively near and the sufferer is dependent on others for care.

It is usually in the second stage that most can be done to prepare for death, saying goodbye, putting things that are wrong right where possible, giving thanks, thinking about what your life has meant. This is the time when psychological help or counseling can be most helpful both for the sufferer and their main carers. It is often a time of relative stability with only slow deterioration, so there is time for such things. It can also be a time of acute fear or of denial (I feel better, I think I am on the mend now). This is almost certainly because of good symptom control.

The control of symptoms

A symptom is simply the way we know we are ill. It is the result of a problem in one or more of our body systems, an imbalance in the body function. Symptoms and their increase or decrease effectively monitor what is happening within our bodies. There are many kinds of symptoms and they can easily be misunderstood for something else which is why medical investigation of any abnormality we are experiencing is urgent.

The discovery of what the meaning of a symptom actually is can be complex. Taking pain as an example, what happens is that the nervous system picks up that something is wrong through its pain fibres. This data is then sent to the brain, which works out where the problem is and logs the sensation as pain. The individual then has to ask what this might mean. How someone thinks about the arrival of pain may depend a lot on his or her current situation. Let's consider two examples. The first is an athlete in training. The second an older woman who has just returned home from an outpatient review of her earlier breast cancer.

The athlete has been over-training. The pain is severe and she is frustrated and angry about it, thinking she may have pulled a hamstring, which is an occupational hazard for her. The pain seems rather severe, however, for that. The athlete worries about a period of lost training, a hiccough in her career, missing a competition.

The older woman had a neighbour who recently died of breast cancer that had, before her death, resulted in extensive secondary deposits in her bones. Thus for her thigh pain has a wholly different meaning. She wonders if her cancer is taking over despite the reassurance from her doctor that things are going very well.

Each person responds to a symptom in line with his or her experience. The reactions can be accurate, or jumbled, or too pessimistic. In both the cases above each person had made a wrong interpretation of what might be happening. The athlete felt she was suffering from over strain; in fact she had a bone cancer and died. The older woman was right in thinking it could have meant her cancer had spread, but it was not so in her case. She had simply cracked a bone.

The interpretation of symptoms reflects a difference in the approach of the doctor and the sufferer. The sufferer wants to know the meaning and implications of the symptom. The doctor will be more interested in the mechanics of what is happening. The implications are unclear to the doctor until the cause has been checked and the questions as to whether it can be treated have been decided. This conflict is not important when the sufferer goes to the doctor who diagnoses and treats the underlying cause after some investigation. The problem goes away, both parties are happy. In incurable illness difficulties can arise as both parties struggle to come to terms with what is happening, the doctor asking what needs to be done for relief now, the sufferer what is going to happen to him or her.

With these differences in mind we can now look at symptoms and how they might be handled.

Management of pain

Up to seventy per cent of terminally ill people experience pain. The intensity of pain usually increases as death nears. The control of pain, in line with the sufferer's experience of it, is probably the most important factor for the dying person. The management of pain has to take account of two factors: the kind of pain being experienced and the growing intensity of it as the illness progresses.

What kind of pain it is influences the best way to manage it. There are three kinds of pain a sufferer may be feeling. These are known clinically as nocioceptic pain, neuropathic pain, and ideopathic or psychological pain.

Nocioceptic pain arises when damage is caused to organs containing nocioceptors. Nocioceptors are widely distributed in skin, muscles, connective tissue and viscera. What they do is send a warning to the brain that damage is occurring. The warning is continuous and increases in intensity as more nocioceptors are affected by the spread of the disease. This kind of pain can be controlled in ninety per cent of cases by the use of drugs including, at later stages, opiates.

Neuropathic pain is caused by damage to the nerves. This means aberrant messages are being sent to the brain and the brain interprets the aberration as pain. Neuropathic pain is more difficult to treat than nociopathic as it responds less well to drugs, including opiates. High dosage opiates are often required and occasionally, in severe cases, a procedure to block the nerves can be used, which prevents transmission of the sensation of pain to the brain.

Ideopathic or psychological pain is more difficult to treat and more controversial. Some pain reported by patients is inexplicable in terms of the known pathology of the disease, or disproportionate to it. This means that it must be the sufferer's own reactions to illness influencing how they experience pain. Despair, helplessness, depression can make pain feel much worse. I experienced this myself. I had to go down to the operating theatre for a third procedure many weeks after my operation. This made me despair, feel afraid, whereas in earlier times I had been more positive. The result was I felt much more sensitive to simple things like the administration of an anaesthetic, which previously I had not been bothered by.

It is sometimes true that psychological pain can be the result of fear of death or of further suffering or lost potential or a feeling of incompleteness. Often simple reassurance or a clear explanation of a situation can relieve this. Sometimes drugs can help such as hypnotics or anxiolytics.

The need to make distinctions between different types of pain in order to treat the sufferer correctly shows how important it is to listen to the patient carefully, have a full history of the illness and to be aware that pain breakthrough can be influenced by how the patient feels.

In terminal cancer for example, pain is commonly caused by the spread of the tumour that triggers more nocioceptors, which registers increased pain in the brain. The tumour can also invade the nerves, causing neuropathic pain as well. Blockage of the lymph system can occur leading to painful edema and, more commonly, constipation, which occurs because of tumour spread. This means the control of pain is a complex matter requiring skill and experience to find the right analgesic mix.

The analgesic ladder in pain management

The process of increasing the dosage of analgesics as an illness progresses is called the analgesic ladder. It is a one-way ladder going only upwards. Best practice is to start as low down the ladder as the condition allows and increase pain relief as needed. It is not generally advisable to provide higher levels of pain relief than required.

Pain-killing drugs are divisible into three levels depending on their strength. The three kinds of pain-killer available are non-opiates, weak opiates and strong opiates. As the type of drug used for pain relief varies the development of the illness is indicated. The different kinds of pain-relieving drugs are not mixed: you are either on non-opiates or weak opiates, codeine phosphate for example, or high opiates, morphine or piperitum (a morphine substitute).

Pain relief has to be used regularly at such intervals as may best minimize the experience of pain. If painkillers are not used regularly or at the right intervals the sufferer becomes anxious and fearful and can deteriorate faster as a result. I know that as I developed gout and was in more constant pain I felt less and less able to cope with everything else.

One thing that is particularly important is for the doctor to react quickly to increases in the pain level. The transition from one level of pain relief to another higher level can be acutely distressing for the sufferer, especially if the doctor is slow to provide the additional relief. This emphasizes the importance of communication between sufferer, medical professionals and carers.

High-level pain relief usually involves morphine and there are some fears about using it, effective though it is. Morphine can produce side effects, for example by stimulating endorphins in the opioid system it can lead to either vomiting or constipation. It does of course cause drowsiness and general lethargy, although this may also be due to physical weakness in general.

Morphine is useful in controlling a wide range of symptoms besides pain. It is also, used properly, safe. People fear morphine addiction and it is known it can kill. It is raw heroin that is addictive and while morphine is made from heroin it does not seem to be addictive where sufferers are prescribed it for pain relief. This fact is well confirmed by studies of sufferers on the drug. As regards morphine shortening life, it can reduce respiration and this is a side effect that has to be monitored carefully.

What we know is that morphine is very effective for pain relief, that people very quickly become acclimatized to it, although strangely not as regards pain relief. In fact people in pain have very aroused nervous systems and this very arousal protects the breathing centre from the negative effects morphine can have. The risks in using it are thus small.

Nausea and vomiting

About sixty per cent of people, as an illness progresses, experience nausea and vomiting. This is either because of the body's reaction to the disease itself, or from the side effects of 'curative' treatments such as chemotherapy or inevitable side effects of the pain control drugs used. Anti-nausea drugs are prescribed to control the condition and are effective in about ninety per cent of cases.

Breathlessness and cough

These are common symptoms particularly in the later stages of an illness. Morphine is used to give relief, as are various other drugs. An inhaled anaesthetic can also relieve blockage of the airways. Breathlessness and cough are caused by the increasing accumulation of fluid in the airways which the body fails to expel.

Appetite and weight loss

Appetite and weight loss occur in the majority of terminally ill people. This is one of the most noticeable things about terminal illness and carers often express concern about it and a wish to rectify it. In the case of dying people it is not just that they are not eating regularly or sufficiently – processes that are taking place in the sufferer's body actually cause weight loss. Depression can also lead to an unwillingness to eat, as can anticipation of nausea. Not too much can be done to reverse this process but gentle encouragement to eat even small nutritious portions can help. A dietician is often helpful.

Mobility and exhaustion

Most dying people experience reduced mobility and exhaustion, especially in the later stages of illness. They are in fact the inevitable consequences of a progressive illness, but they have to be coped with practically. An occupational therapist can often help with physical aids such as walking frames or through showing how something can be more easily done. The least effort the better for an exhausted person. I used to sit on the side of my bed and wonder how I was going to have the energy to pull my trousers on; I could sit for half an hour before I summoned up enough strength and will to do so. Eventually a sufferer does not want to turn over in bed and tries not to cough; it is all too much.

Constipation

Once someone becomes less active and particularly when they are bed bound they become constipated and it worsens as time passes. If the waste accumulates in the system other complications can arise. For example the bowel contents can become very hard and impacted and this results in copious and foul vomiting. Constipation can, however, be relieved quickly and effectively either with laxatives or with enemas.

Mood changes

Quite a few patients suffer from altered mood. This can be the result of untreated depression but it also can be the result of the underlying disease. For example tumours that spread to the brain can change the personality or the mood. Strokes have the same effect.

Oral discomfort and pressure sores

Many patients develop oral discomfort due to dryness and sores in the mouth. These are the result of dehydration and inadequate nutrition. It is essential to keep the mouth clean and wet to relieve this symptom.

Common pressure sores (bedsores) can also be a problem as can infected lesions or necrotic skin sores. These can all become malodorous if left untreated, adding to a person's anxiety and sense of self-disgust. Treatment is with anti-fungal creams and sometimes with antibiotics. It is usually effective but nursing care is needed to keep the sores clean.

Accumulating symptoms

To me the very worst thing about dying was the accumulation of symptoms. It seemed like one thing after another. How much could I take? To breathlessness was added gout, skin lesions, itching, and sleeplessness, vomiting and physical weakness. Life became a kind of nightmare; you lived from one physical crisis to another. You had to retreat into a corner of yourself to cope with it. That meant pushing the world away as much as you could. At the same time you were trying to carry on and not let people know how bad it was for you, even feeling guilty about it. I felt very alone; there was no help and no-one to talk to except my wife whom I was trying to make feel I was not so bad. In good palliative care nurses and physiotherapists help but I wonder how many dying people felt and feel as alone as I did.

Conclusion

As you die you become less independent and more dependent upon those around you. You face a kind of disintegration or dissolution as your systems fail, as the symptoms accumulate. Despair and depression are frequent companions, yet you have to try and stay in control because you know once you lose control, you have had it. This was as far as I got. In the next chapter I will try to explain what happens in the last forty-eight hours or so of life, the terminal hours which thankfully are still in the future for me. Let us all remember though, this will be part of our future.

Chapter 3

The Last Days
and Death Itself

It is the last days and hours that seem to present carers, rather than the dying person, with the greatest time of anxiety, not necessarily because death itself is close but because of the fear that something unexpected, unpleasant or distressing is suddenly going to occur. Most carers have developed routines that help them cope and, of course, it is very stressful to watch someone you care for suffer and approach death. From this comes the fear that they may not be able to cope with sudden and unexpected changes or increased suffering for the patient. Practical advice and reassurance is needed to explain what is happening and what is likely to happen as well as the knowledge that extra help will quickly be available.

The dying person also expresses fears as they sense the end is near. The fears are not so much about what will happen as most have asked about this before or decided they do not want to know, or feel reconciled to their coming death. The anxiety is often that they will be alone when they die, particularly at the actual moment of death. This may be just a fear reaction, as it is natural not to want to go into the unknown alone. Some people do not have anyone they are close to however, or those caring for them may be afraid to be there when the death actually occurs. This is a fear that we need to be aware of and respond to, to see that someone of importance to the patient is, if at all possible, around the patient all the time.

There is little written about what happens to a person in the last hours of their life. It is nevertheless a natural process occurring to us and as Marcus Aurelius said, referring to the stoic philosophy

'I am a man, nothing human is foreign to me.'

What are the the changes that show death may be near?

Indicators that death is imminent

- The person is largely confined to bed or to an armchair or couch. This will be because the patient is by this time either so wasted and exhausted that he or she loses all interest in movement, or because movement may cause pain or vomiting.

- The person will have lost interest in day-to-day matters and seems to be living in a separate world, even resenting disturbance for such things as drug administration or washing.

- The person will lose interest in eating and drinking. This is common but not universal. It is not uncommon for something like a 'Big Mac' to be consumed with gusto within a day of death. However, for the majority swallowing becomes too difficult and exhausting a few days before death. Eating and drinking become irrelevant to the dying person.

- Changes occur in breathing rhythms. This is perhaps the clearest indicator that death is near.

- Most people spend most of their time sleeping or semi-awake. It is hard to know if the person is asleep or awake most of the time and if he or she is at all aware of what is happening around him or her.

Last stage palliation

The most important aim of any treatment in the last few days of life is to relieve all symptoms so the person can die without pain or other problems, particularly vomiting.

In the last days the dying person may need medication for symptom relief but cannot swallow easily. As a result drugs may need to be given into the rectum or, more often, subcutaneously. Thus many people who are near death will have been fitted with a continuous infusion device known as a syringe driver. This injects contents of 10ml over a twenty-four hour period and means that cocktails of analgesics, anti-emetics and sedatives can be given safely and without disturbing the patient. The main change is that palliation is increased to the point that symptoms are fully controlled and the provision of care is made as unobtrusive as possible to maintain the dying person's peacefulness.

Communication

Most dying people seem to remain aware of their surroundings right up until death. They just have no energy to respond to them. There are many cases that report consciousness continuing during anaesthesia and of what are termed 'near death experiences'. Some people can recount in detail events and conversations that took place during periods of unconsciousness and it is well known that unconscious people often react to their surroundings. The arrival of a person in the room, or the presence of some conflict can be reflected in agitation in someone who appears comatose.

It seems best, therefore, for relatives and friends to talk as normally as possible around the dying person and, if they feel it is appropriate, to take the opportunity to say whatever last things they need or wish to say to the dying person. It is also a good time to show love, affection and reassurance but not false reassurance that assures the person of recovery. Professional carers attending the person also need to talk to them as they go about their practical tasks, telling the person what they are doing, how they are doing it and offering the usual pleasantries and news. It is, of course, obviously important that people take care not to talk about matters that may raise anxiety and to ensure the patient does not overhear discussions about their coming death.

The aim is not just to keep the dying person as comfortable as possible but to continue to show they are a real person, able to be included in what is happening around them, worthy of displays of affection and care. This helps maintain the person's dignity and self-worth in a time of suffering and dissolution.

Holding on and letting go when the death time is prolonged

The strength of human ties can be seen in the starkest way at the time of death. The strength of these ties seems to influence the time of death in many cases. There seems to be a choice for some people to hold on a bit longer or to let go. Many people remain alive until a particular person has been to see them or until a particular event has taken place, perhaps a birthday or an anniversary. The dying person wants to see that person or be part of that event before they will let go.

Some dying people seem to need permission to die. They respond to fears that their loved ones often express such as 'I don't know what I'll do when you are gone' or the more plaintive and desperate cries of 'don't go' or 'please don't leave me'. No matter how much the dying person has resolved his personal business or reconciled herself with her coming death people who are dying often hold on for the sake of their loved ones. They may hate the thought of a long parting from those they deeply love.

Thus sometimes a dying person needs permission to let go. As has been said 'she needs to know it's all right to die now' and 'he needs to be told he can go'. When reassurance is given by loved ones or by people the dying person trusts, perhaps a doctor or nurse, then they often do let go.

Sometimes the dying person may simply be still afraid to die – although most people seem ready to go; they have suffered enough. In such cases, however, it helps to talk to the person and give as much reassurance as possible that all will be forgiven and all will be at peace in the time to come. However the reassurer must genuinely believe this.

A few people seem just not to be ready to give in and want to fight to the bitter end. As one person who had lain half conscious for nearly six weeks said 'why should I go, you are a long time dead, every moment of life is precious, hard or not'. In these cases eventually resistance fails and the patient's attitude implies that not everything was done while the patient was well enough to prepare for death.

Death itself

Death itself is not an event in the usual sense of the word. There is, of course, a moment when a person becomes a corpse, perhaps when breathing ceases or brain activity ends. But in all but death from immediate trauma the parting is more a prolonged leaving than an abrupt exit. Some cultures recognize this by insisting that a body is not moved for some hours after death, until the changes are plain and inexorable. In the West we define death in terms of different categories of brain death and have certain procedures that certify death has taken place. For example ensuring the eyes are fixed and the pupils dilated.

However, the diagnosis that a death has occured needs to be a careful one. There are some very well-publicized cases where people who have been thought to have been dead have suddenly sat up on the mortuary slab. The transition is mostly clear but care needs to be taken to ensure the person is really dead and their body now a corpse. Fortunately there are some very observable changes in a person in the hours leading up to death. These are:

1. Changes in breathing. These usually begin a few hours before death or occasionally a few days before and take several forms. The reason for these changes is not that the person is struggling or too weak to breathe normally, but rather that the cycles of breathing are by now being controlled by very primitive reflexes or by chemical changes in the body that are accompanying the death. There is no evidence at this stage that the dying person is aware of the changes in their breathing or of breathing at all, as from physiological research, breathing driven by chemical changes seems not to lead to breathlessness.

2. Chest secretions. As breathing becomes shallow, the dying person will tend not to cough or clear their throat, thus not moving the secretions we all swallow automatically and clear by clearing

our throats or coughing. Any small pool of se-
cretion that accumulates in either the throat or
the airways will vibrate as breathing continues
creating a noise like a gargle. Clinically it is ut-
terly inconsequential but it has led to the grue-
some label of 'death rattle' being applied to it.
These chest secretions can be dried up using
hyoscine. If pneumonia is present then reducing
temperature with paracetomol or steroid and
giving a small amount of opiate or sedative if
the person appears breathless or distressed as-
sists. Suffice it to say that when secretions do
accumulate in this way this is a sign that death
is probable in no more than a day or two.

3. Usually those around the dying person know. It
   seems that most carers in close proximity or
   regularly attending a dying person somehow
   recognize when the time has come and a person
   is actually dying. This is probably because they
   notice, without necessarily understanding, the
   changes in the person's breath or attitude.

The most common way of knowing that death has actually occurred is to observe that breathing has ceased and
the pupils of the eyes have become fixed and dilated.
The mouth also sometimes falls open as the jaw muscles
relax. Heartbeat and pulse cease and over a period of
time the body temperature falls and rigor mortis sets in
as the blood coagulates in the veins and arteries.

Aftermath

This book is not about grief, but grief is present among the family and friends of the dying person before the actual death, usually beginning once it is known that death will be the result.

A death remains in the minds of those who shared the experience with the dying person. It has a profound effect not just in terms of a sense of grief and bereavement, though these may be overwhelming experiences, at least at first. It is terrible to lose someone you love.

Sometimes the experience has been powerful and full of suffering, and grief continues after the death, so that we may not learn all we can from the dying time of those we know. What follows is a consideration of my own experiences of people approaching death and the experiences of people I knew or met who died and the circumstances and suffering that led to their death.

Chapter 4

How Dying People Feel about Death and Dying

In my experience there was no hard and fast moment when I realized I was dying and had to deal with that coming reality. Rather it was an awareness that grew inside me, one that a hopeful day could dissipate, until such days became few in number. My experience of working with people in the process of dying also suggested this was their experience. I used to think it was a kind of denial of the inevitable, a refusal to accept a situation that was obvious to me as a therapist. I was wrong, I realized, when I came to have the experience myself.

Awareness of your coming death is a process that grows in certainty as your conditions worsen. A process often interrupted by new hopes of certain treatments, good palliation so you feel less ill and the sheer enormity of the event you are anticipating, your end. It is just not possible to conceive what death will be like, nor the final days of life. I knew intellectually, of course, because I had seen the last days of dying people often, but I came to understand that it was one thing to observe physically how it happened, another actually to experience it. You could not anticipate it because you could not comprehend it.

Awareness of death

I think I experienced my encounter with death in four stages and from remembering the experiences of others I had seen dying these seem at least general if not particular in every case. The first stage is coming to know you have a life-threatening condition and that if treatment fails you will face death. At this time you have a vague inner realization of the physical problem you are facing; you feel something is wrong, but it does not yet feel likely to be fatal. As a result, and as a consequence of medical optimism and advice, you focus on getting better, on defeating the illness or at the very least preventing its further development. With a cardio-myopathy such as my own, there is no hope of treatment unless you can get on a transplant list. Given that there are thousands on the list and only about two hundred transplants a year, access to the only curative treatment is unlikely. You must concentrate on slowing down the progress of the disease by the use of heart-assisting drugs. With other illnesses, such as, cancer, treatment is comparatively short and unpleasant but the prognosis is more hopeful.

The next stage comes untidily for two reasons. A realization that treatment is failing, and some inner voice telling you things are worse. This leads to a period of acute anxiety and fear, and also a need to press for treatment and relief. It is a time when the dialogue between the doctors, carers and patient hardens, becomes more fraught and anxious for all of them. I came to understand that, after a few years of successful control of my symptoms, they had begun to worsen. Something told me to seek more help and it was hard to accept that little could be done; deterioration had set in and was likely to escalate.

There is a danger in this time that the patient may make requests for additional treatment that cannot really help and may in fact cause greater suffering. This was certainly so in my own case. The cardiologist responded by changing my treatment to a new more experimental drug, which was sheer torture and had the opposite effect to what was intended. Carers too press for action, worry the patient by pushing them to demand more care and affect the climate of anxiety around the patient. Medical professionals will also want to help; that is what they are for. They hate to lose a patient; rightly so. Nevertheless they can tend to concentrate on continuing curative attempts when pallia-tion is more helpful.

In the end, however, nothing can prevent the onset of the third stage. Here is the inner realization that death is now inevitable – and the need for treatment to be confined mostly to palliation. I call this time the 'waiting room' time. The angel of death has not called you but you know the call is imminent. Most people try to stay as well as they can during this time, and live as normal a life as their symptoms allow and palliative care can ensure. Psychologically it involves a review of your life, a wondering about what it has meant, if anything, a sense of futility, a measure of anger against cruel fate and a need to know others still care about you despite your condition. It was in this period I said my good-byes, tried to put right wrong things, said thank you and worked for a good ending. It was a very satisfying, even emotionally confirming, activity and I am glad I always advised my patients in the past to do this. It helps towards acceptance and peace.

Finally you become aware of multiplying symptoms, increasing physical weakness, lack of interest in anything worldly and some real pain and discomfort. Even then I wanted to linger as long as possible; death was inevitable but not here yet. It was a shock to know how near it was. Most patients slide into this period, become bed or chair ridden, lose interest in the world and live a kind of inward existence which is hard to explain. I used to tell relatives, friend and carers to tell the patient everything, keep them up to date even though they might not respond. This was good advice I think. It helps the person feel loved and included at the end. It was certainly important to me. What was not so good was the suggestion the patient be kept as active as possible, try to take nutrition, to wash, and so on. This seems to me now to be foolish; what I appreciated was help with all those things, not being forced to do them.

I did not go to the end of this road — a little miracle occurred for me; but I went far enough to see how it was. I noticed when I was working with dying people that in that last dying time they often came to acceptance and wisdom. One patient turned to his son and said 'all will be well, you can rely on that'. Simple but wonderful as, in extremity, he tried to reassure his distressed son. Or the woman, who was dying alone, who said to me, holding up her head a little, 'It has been a good life on the whole. How fortunate I am, I can go in peace.'

A sense of separation

To me — both personally and as a counselor — one of the most striking factors of dying was the sense you had of separation from the world. In a way you inhabited two worlds. One was the ordinary day-to-day world where death was growing inside you but you coped with the ordinary things as best you could. You slowly adjusted to the idea you needed more help and became reconciled to the loss of independence. In this world you could see friends, read newspapers but all the time with a growing sense of unreality. How I regretted leaving it, but at the same time did not want to stay.

There was a second world as well. It was a world inside myself, an awareness of dissolution and ending. You could not have explained this world to others; it was vivid, full of remembrance and imagination and at the same time sad. I thought about the meaning of my life, sought solace. In my case I wanted to have the last rites of the Catholic Church of which I am properly an agnostic member. Yet in the face of death I became more religious, seeking some bridge between life and death. 'Holy Mary', I would say often, 'pray for us sinners, now and at the hour of our death'.

I know that many people who are dying feel much the same though they express it in different ways. Thomas More, who was executed by Henry VIII, wrote as he awaited his beheading, 'death wonderfully focuses the mind' and this is certainly true. You come to think only of the things important to you and of the questions of meaning.

So many of my cases come to mind in this respect. There was the case of an Irish man dying of bowel cancer in his forties. His wife was caring for him. The trouble was he had been a bad husband, getting drunk, often beating her and the children. She had left him but had come back to be with him in his final days. He lived longer than expected, seemingly unwilling to let go. She maintained her outward caring but she hurt him in all sorts of ways, like pressing his bedsores and complaining continually to him. He was really paying for how he had treated her. Attempts to move him into care, however, failed. 'I'm having my hell now', he told me, 'and this will be time off in the after life'. I wondered if he was just being difficult. 'I deserve it all', he told me, 'when I let go it will be when I've paid'. In the end he took to the whisky again.

A woman dying of esophageal cancer fought against it, determined to beat it, long after it had progressed beyond all hope. When doctors failed her she turned to homeopaths, astrologers and angels she claimed to have seen. Things worsened nevertheless and finally she was bed ridden and knew she was near the end. Even then she bullied her husband unmercifully as to how she wanted to be cared for. One day, a few days before she died, she said to me 'When did I die do you think?' I was a bit bewildered. 'You haven't died yet', I said. 'So you say' she said, 'I've tried not to'. I asked her what she meant. 'Everything seems so unreal', she went on, 'I must be dead'. Her battle against death ended with a realization she had died long before as the person she saw herself.

Gavin was only twenty and was dying of an AIDS-related illness. He had been very angry about this happening to him and then apathetic. He just lay on his bed silently and let his partner and his mother do the necessary caring. He was conscious, appeared benevolent, but gave every sign of absence. All this was not happening to him, he was somewhere else and he was I think in his imagination. Just before he died his mother told me he opened his eyes, saw her and his partner, smiled and said 'O this place is still here'. She said his eyes were very intense and full of awareness. 'I must be going' he said as he fell into his last coma.

I am not sure what all this means or tells us. It just happened to others and me. We moved away from the world, the world became less real. I wrote my funeral poem for a friend to read out at the funeral mass during this last time. It shows the leaving.

> *When I see the mountains on the other side of the moon,*
> *I shall know I have left this beautiful pebble*
> *That confined me long and held me close,*
> *And I shall rejoice and be glad*
> *And look outwards,*
> *Ready to sail the stellar winds.*
>
> *Do not grieve for me those who remain*
> *On the lustful and effulgent earth,*
> *I am free and you must endure again*

The long years of entropy
In that uncertain place.

I go on the great adventure
The earth prepared me for
Free from the sheer profusion of devourment
The earth so beautifully allows
And in some exaltation of the spirit
I shall begin my real existence.

Inner questions

I think the common questions considered by dying people, apart from how they will die and what relief they will have, are inward ones about various kinds of meaning. Even if people do not articulate the questions in the form used here they are questions common among dying people. Maybe this isn't surprising. If you are leaving something, then you want to see what it meant at the time and for the future.

Questions of suffering

Why do we suffer? This simple question is quite complex. What do we mean by suffering? It seems to include two themes. The first is physical suffering where pain stimuli are hard to control or where other symptoms like diarrhea leave you exhausted and dehydrated. Then there is something we call mental suffering exhibited in its worst forms in depression, anxiety states and mental illness. Of course one can be affected or even caused by the other, but there is a crucial difference in kind between these two experiences.

Religiously inclined people or believers in God wonder about the apparent contradiction between an idea of benevolent creation and the suffering world. 'How can God permit such misery' or 'what have I done to deserve this'. There is no clear answer. Maybe God is benevolent in ways we do not understand.

Pain, devourment and I guess suffering seem to be a normal part of the way the universe works. Everything that comes into being eventually suffers entropy and death; it is the way things are. We may be able to delay the process, inhibit it, and reduce its effects as far as some things are concerned, but the process appears natural and inevitable. The Buddha recognized this in his Great Noble Truths where he makes us face the fact that sorrow and dealing with it is a key part of learning to live well.

It is not surprising we find it hard to accept that suffering is a natural part of experience. It is unpleasant, dangerous and life-diminishing. It is part of the conflict between our instinct to try and survive and the inevitability of death. There must be someone to blame for it, maybe God, doctors, food suppliers, the weather, our own foolishness, whatever. There is usually some blaming of some kind by dying people for the fact they are dying. I personally got very angry at what I then saw as the neglect of the cardiologists at the Birmingham hospital, believing that neglect hastened my decline. I think now they were less attentive than they might have been but it seems unlikely that it made much difference.

Guilt is also part of a dying person's suffering. Guilt that you are ill and causing concern and hard work for others. Guilt that your own carelessness about your health might have been a factor in getting the illness – smoking, obesity, lack of exercise for example. This guilt contains a fear that we deserve our fate and that carers might be angry with us.

Guilt is also a factor for those watching a person die. They feel guilty because they cannot do more, or ashamed of their distaste for the situation, the mess. This leads to all sorts of dramatic interventions in care or the search for treatment that is often in fact bad for the dying person, but the watcher feels better for doing something.

Suffering can seem pointless, prolonged, cruel and unnecessary. It can dehumanize us. There is a point where pain or other problems can overwhelm our ability to cope with it. This is why some people incline to euthanasia and why we have to have palliation, that is relief of symptoms.

Some people feel suffering is a kind of test of faith or character. They struggle to overcome the challenge to demonstrate their strength of will. I myself found it humiliating, disgusting and it made me angry. I could have punched God on the nose and asked if he couldn't, being omnipotent, have found a better way for people to die. I don't know what I expected but needless to say the feeling changed nothing. So you end up asking for mercy.

Suffering increases with time in terminal illness, even if symptoms are well controlled. It is also a form of suffering to be aware of your sedation and dependence; it makes you know you are dying. You cannot go altogether quietly into that good night. One young man put up a valiant fight against severe burns, but eventually he lost the battle and was dying. He was suffering greatly and increasingly every day he lived. Even his brother, whom he confronted with a confession of deep betrayal, said 'You wouldn't want a demon to die like this' and told him that he had forgiven him.

Another man who was on renal dialysis felt the very slow deterioration in his quality of life and the effect on that of his wife and to a lesser extent his children served no point. Shortly after his last daughter's marriage he decided to have no more dialysis. This means death in ten to fifteen days. He could not be persuaded out of it; he had had enough, saw no point in being a burden on others any more. He died eleven days later with his family around him. Here the gradual accretion of suffering led to a person choosing to die.

In practical terms there are a few things that have to be done about suffering. They are:

1. Make sure that all that can be done to relieve pain and symptoms clinically and practically has been done.

2. Provide appropriate help to enable the dying person to discuss the inner questions that concern them.

3. Cope with greater dependence, or with carers' greater need to care.

There is one other aspect of suffering to be considered. Can it be transcended? We cannot transcend it physically; we are in the process of dying, and we can delay it a bit, or help it a bit, but not change it. Many people do, however, find a sense of acceptance both of the extent of their suffering and of their general situation. Some even begin to anticipate a life beyond. We admire such people. I remember I felt deeply touched by a young man dying unpleasantly of an AIDS-related illness. He called his friends and family together one day because he was worried about their reactions to his pain and coming death. He quite bluntly told them to get on with their lives, thanked them for their help and said it was no use regretting him or his life as he had enjoyed it and was ready now to leave. I found it helped the dying person to express concern for those caring and to try to lessen the unhappiness of their families and friends at the prospect. I certainly wanted to do that, because I realized how much I was demanding above the norm.

I have come to the conclusion suffering just is. You can do something to relieve it, but you cannot avoid it. It is no good complaining about it. The only thing to do is learn to live with it and, of course, to die with it.

Fate

Most people ask, 'why me'. I asked it and a friend told me 'would you complain if you won the lottery?' I saw his point, fate takes a hand, things good as well as bad happen as if out of the blue. This answered the question for me, but it is more difficult with others.

'I am angry this has happened to me', a patient told me, 'I don't deserve it'. Does anyone I wondered, trying to explain to him that while that might be true it didn't alter anything. He sued his doctor anyway.

Fate seems to intervene a lot in life. I remember standing in front of the memorial arch at Ypres and seeing the names of the thousands of young men who had died at the various battles there about. Battles that changed nothing and were often just killing grounds. I saw an uncle's name written there; he was only twenty. Did they ask why this was happening to them? Most seem to have volunteered for love of country or adventure. Maybe when they were about to die there was also courage and hope for that reason. To those of us coming afterwards it seems such a terrible waste. Death is a waste when it is untimely.

Meaning

'Did my life mean anything?' I asked myself one day sitting in some gardens looking at spring flowers. Many dying people have asked me 'what has it all been for?' It is as if, if you lived longer, you might find out! When my aunt of 89 asked me I realized the question was existential. 'What do you think it was about?' I countered defensively.

'Sex and good times', she replied unexpectedly and rather out of character. 'This is why I am ready to go now dear, no sex, too ill for good times.' This from a woman who clung on to life because she said she was afraid what God might say to her about her sins. She had her last lover in her early eighties.

I suppose the inability to do one's thing is a way to lose meaning. After all we have, these days, mostly chosen what we are doing so it must be meaningful to us. To lose it is to be down or depressed. That is at one level. At another the question is a much larger one.

Stephen was a man in his thirties dying of a cancer. He was often in black despair not because of the illness but because he felt his life had been useless to him and anyone else. He claimed he had been a failure in career, relationships, and education and was a real outsider. It was true his life had not been successful in all those areas. 'You might as well not have had me', he told his mother with typical tact.

It was hard to get carers to go and see him, not to mention his parents. He filled people with black despair, almost had a talent for it. So one day, exasperated, I said 'Hell's teeth Steve, you go on, you must know what your life has been about'. 'Oh I do', he said, 'it is just not enough'. 'Well what?' I asked. 'Just being alive changes the world around you', he replied, 'God knows how, but it does'. I told him that was all too true – he was making everyone depressed. 'They'll live', he said pointedly.

One old man I sat with ruminated like this. He was dying of cancer but felt he had enjoyed a long and happy life; even so he was wondering what it had been for. His answer was unusual and profound: he concluded one could not know and that was good. He felt the mere fact we had existed changed the story of existence. 'I suppose', he said, 'I just changed the story of existence a bit and my kids are continuing the work'. There is much meaningful in children, they give strength to your own being by offering meaning in terms of the future. This man saw the universe as a process in which possibilities were explored; just to have been a part of that process, one of its possibilities, was enough for him.

After death

Dying people often ask, 'Do you think there is an afterlife?' I have no idea of course; I rather hope there is. Some people affirm an afterlife, really believe in one, and seem to live for it. Others think the final end has come. Some, like me, just hope for the best.

A large black woman dying of cancer gave her testimony, as she called it, to her pastor when I was visiting also. She gave the testimony with all her heart; you knew she believed it and because of that it was beautiful. She said:

> 'I am going to the Lord Jesus, to his bosom as he promised. I know nobody ever came back to tell he was waiting, as he said he would, but He is calling me like a shining light. Not in this old body, He ain't, but down there inside of me where me and my Lord meet now and again, but soon forever.'

Or this from a young man dying too soon.

> 'It seems hopeless to be leaving life out of season. Going too soon. I am angry about it, I feel denied my birthright. Somehow, however, this is not the end. I can't say why. It is not

because of all the crap you hear about the afterlife. It is something deep down at a point I seem to be more than me.'

This sense that within was a place where we met the universe I have met in various forms many times with dying people. It is also something I felt myself. I do not know whether it is just psychology or that bit of our genes that makes us believers, but I do know the feeling is very real, troubling as well as inspiring. I know I thought 'goodness, there is really something after all'.

Religious teachings have all sorts of tomorrows to offer and always have had. The truth we afford those teachings is, however, a matter of personal faith. One thing religion seems to be about is living this life in the hope of a better life to come or in preparation for such a reward.

I suppose it is impossible to know objectively if there is life after death. We can believe there is and act on that belief, as I did when I asked the Catholic Church to give me the last rites, yet the doubt remained. It is, I think, harder than atheists like to admit to imagine a complete ending, to feel nothing of us continues. Our instincts are for life. Maybe this is why I felt, as I neared death, that the universe and I were becoming one; in other words I was merging back into the environment. This reinforced my long-held view that as we are a product of the universe we must hold within some echo or residue of the creative force that began existence. This gave me great hope when I was dying.

'I do not know' one woman wrote to me, 'if my life has meant anything or if I shall live on in some new form. What I do know is that God is with me, if God is the right word. I am connected to everything, therefore I have received the miracle of being.'

Or perhaps more simply as a 32-year-old man said to his friend just before he died:

> 'I am going now Jack. See you on the other side one day. That is my promise to you. It is where the sun really shines.'

Chapter 5

Thoughts About Life, Death and Dying

The care of the dying and the experience of being a dying person raises profound issues about life and death. Not least is the much debated matter of euthanasia or the right to die. In some ways that issue both focuses and obscures some of the other matters that need thought and I will return to this later in the book. In this chapter I want to set out the ethical problems that I encountered myself in the process of dying, and that I observed and participated in when caring for dying people. Euthanasia is only one of the problems.

Suffering

In earlier chapters we looked at suffering from a purely physical point of view. In this chapter we look at the issues of care and comfort it raises. Suffering can mean different things in each circumstance.

For example one can argue that a woman in childbirth suffers probably as much as anyone is likely to encounter. The total experience is, however, usually very positive. The suffering is experienced because of greater rewards. To a lesser extent this is true of the person in temporary discomfort after successful surgery or treatment. The result is positive; the discomfort is worth it. In contrast there is the person who is dying. Here, suffering is an indication of the progress of the terminal condition, it can fill with fear and dread, and it has no positive outcome. Thus there is a connection in the morale of the patient between likely outcome and endurance.

When a person is dying, there are considerations for them and for everyone about the process of dying and its impact.

There are four main aspects:

1. A sense of helplessness

2. An increase in the sources of conflict

3. Diminishing sympathy

4. Unresolved issues.

Helplessness

Physical weakness makes us more and more dependent on other people, something that is normally unacceptable outside childhood. Modern society expects us to be independent and healthy. We are in control of ourselves, at least overtly. We get prestige from those things we do well and hide those things where we feel exposed or foolish. We are also able to be private. When we are helpless we are much less able to be private.

For example, a fifty-year-old man has a slight stroke. He is heavily overweight. In hospital he regains full use of his right arm and leg and is discharged knowing it is essential to lose weight. He has to try to control the anxieties and underlying causes of overeating and he can no longer hide these or the fact of his obesity. His suffering is extended because he must diet, face the issues in himself that caused obesity and struggle to overcome them. As he has been ill because of his weight, he can no longer pretend it does not matter that he overeats; he is exposed.

When I was recovering from dying, it was a great relief to have lost 20 kilos as a result of improved control of edema. It made me feel I did not need to change my eating habits as I regained my appetite. The result has been unwelcome weight gain. I am ashamed of it.

The real issue about helplessness is, however, the challenge it makes to the dying person, carers and society in general. Helplessness necessitates care and the acceptance of it. Care takes time and money and generally with dying people will end in a death. Respect for the dying person makes it sensible to limit care to what is needed, enabling a measure of independence as long as possible, but this has to be while taking account of a worsening condition.

Once, years ago, when I was talking to a man dying of cancer and not far from death, he complained that people didn't realize how helpless he was, and wanted him to try and do things he felt unable to do unaided (wash himself for example, or use a bed pan). I myself reached a point where I became impatient at being encouraged to do things (like cook some food or make a drink) which I felt too exhausted to undertake properly. Nevertheless the dying person is also conscious of the strain he or she is putting on those around, and often struggles to hide the level of their dependence. There seems to be a point where a transition takes place and the dying person accepts and needs care and yet is ashamed to reveal the extent of that need.

The care of helpless people requires a commitment to someone and that means there is a financial consideration involved. Professional carers cost money, home carers must have some replacement for lost income. This in itself is a fraught matter of priorities in a resource-scarce environment. A dying person is aware of this.

Some think they will get what they can, others are grateful for what is available, as I was for practical aids offered through occupational therapy.

I remember being very reluctant to use a heightened toilet seat. It raised all sorts of issues for me. Privacy about defecation is rather important. Might a raised seat get dirty, would it look unpleasant, did it mean I could no longer bend, for example, without discomfort? In the end it is continence issues that most demonstrate helplessness and cause dismay to carers. When I was recovering in hospital and had to use a commode and also needed help to wipe myself clean, it was a relief to have nurses' help; trained to do this and to be unfazed by it. I never quite got used to the intimate care it means.

How are we going to deal with the problem of helplessness? Perhaps in an increasingly fragmented society we need to face dependence in the interest of community.

Increasing conflicts

The prospect of death raises new issues about the nature of your life. Quite apart from the struggle to adapt to higher levels of suffering, itself difficult, or to cope with increased dependence, many face some difficult needs to reconcile those things in their lives that are incomplete or unhappy.

Most people, for example, have families on whom to rely. Many in modern times do not. They may have lost contact or there may be no surviving members, a frequent situation among older people. A sense of aloneness can be frightening in such cases, as can the sense of peripherality that results from not being deeply important to someone. Some people have found new social relationships to replace family and these need to be respected and catered for despite the fact that, unless they make a will, their heirs are their remaining biological family, and they may not even know whether any exist. The distress caused by a lack of belonging or centrality to others can be a real source of worry or nervousness for some dying people

The increase in pain or other symptoms, the sense of dissolution, the feeling of dependence and the inevitable review of one's life and significance to others all contribute to the anxiety of the dying person. In addition the person may be afraid of death, or of the last stages now approaching or both. I know I was afraid as to how I would die. I had seen people myself struggling with breath, vomiting and so on and I did not want to go through it. The actual hours of death were less fearful as for the most part, as T.S. Eliot put it in his poem, we die not 'with a bang, but a whimper'.

Anxiety about dying, or what may happen after death, contributes to conflict around the dying person.

In some cases so do the anxieties and stress of the prime carers, who may be finding the job too troubling or physically difficult, too intrusive on their normal lives. A dying person can be aware of this and worried about it.

Diminishing sympathy

The immediate reaction most of us feel to those who are suffering is sympathy, including a desire to help. We have this feeling because we have suffered in some way regardless of whether or not we understand why suffering must exist. We know we will die in future so in every death we anticipate our own as John Donne pointed out in the 17th century:

> 'No man is an Island, entire of itself; every man is a piece of the Continent, a part of the main. If a clod be washed away by the sea, Europe is the less, as well as if a promontory were, as well as if a manor of thy friends or of thine own were: any man's death diminishes me, for I am involved in Mankind, and therefore never send to know for whom the bell tolls; it tolls for thee.'

Sympathy is a complicated matter, however. It might be understood to have a number of dimensions to it. The first might be described as *the will to resolution.* The suffering must be controlled and resolved. The parents of Tim, a nine-year-old child with leukemia, persuaded him to take additional treatments, despite the side effects and low odds. Reflecting on it with hindsight, they wished they had not encouraged him to this extra and, as it turned out, unhelpful suffering. And yet we cannot blame them, they wanted their child to have a life, his anguish resolved positively, not with death. In some senses this was also true of the family of a woman with breast cancer, particularly her husband, who wanted to leave no stone unturned to beat her cancer and to resolve her pain with hope. Almost certainly this increased rather than diminished her suffering, as she had to make a decision not to be treated further against his feelings.

This leads on to the second dimension of sympathy, *the demand that suffering be relieved.* There is a clear and understandable demand by dying people and carers that if the condition cannot be relieved, then the suffering must be. This is the whole basis of the palliative approach. It is not, however, an easy thing to do because, as with Tim, treatment can cause suffering and inhibit relief. A crucial moment for carers and a dying person is when the decision is made to abandon treatment and go for simple relief; it is hard to abandon hope of life or to watch someone you care for die. Nothing upsets more than unrelieved symptoms, and the dying process is fraught with times when palliation may not be quite meeting the new situation caused by the progression of the terminal condition. In those times carers can become very angry and have problems dealing with their feelings.

A third dimension of sympathy is that it *decreases rather than increases with time.* As a carer you can get used to suffering and develop a hard shell to diminish its effect on yourself. A sympathizing person has their own life and that life demands attention, which sympathizing cannot diminish. This leads to an expectation that the suffering person has a duty to cope as best they can and not to intrude too greatly. For the day-to-day carer, this can be a crucial matter; the demands of care increase while the sympathy decreases, and are sometimes overtaken by their own resentment at having to sacrifice more of their own lives than they hoped. Of course this leads to a sense of guilt; you ought not to feel like that, what does it say about you? So these normal feelings are often disguised, or the demand on others that the sufferer be helped is increased, thus compensating for the sense of guilt. The decrease in sympathy is inevitable and normal and the main objective is to live with it as best you can without upsetting the sufferer.

I noticed myself that when I was first ill, everyone came to see me, wanted to know how I was; this was great, it made me feel appreciated. Then as time passed, people got on with their own lives, visited less often, rang less frequently, sort of put me out of their immediate concerns. Fair enough really; all I could do was confront them with the unpleasant realities of dying and these I wanted to keep to myself as much as possible; yet it hurt a little nevertheless.

A final dimension of suffering is *the power it gives to the sympathizer*. The sympathizer can see the effect of their concern and sympathy on the sufferer. As a result the relationship between the sympathizer and the sufferer is changed. Some sympathizers welcome this, feeling more in control of things; others are bewildered by it. For example, a man very dominant in his home was dying of cancer. He became dependent on his wife and was rather afraid. His wife, used to a submissive role in the home, found it hard to accept and deal with her new need to make decisions for the family and about her husband's care. In another case a woman who had been particularly demanding of her children and manipulative of them found herself confronted by their refusal to take on a main caring role; she could not understand what she had done, but her two daughters felt justified in denying her something she needed.

Sympathy is a double edged matter; it demands action, yet increases anxiety and changes over time. I remember my uncle always had a very unsympathetic approach to death, but he could cope with dead bodies. Tackling him about it when my brother died, he said he had seen it all in the trenches in 1917; it held no horrors for him – only the fact that it could happen was distressing.

Unresolved issues

People do not die in a vacuum; their lives have not become complete when they die. This means that there are unresolved issues and these tend to worry dying people.

These are not simply the sort of issues that a young mother faces in realizing she is dying before her children are independent, but also bad memories of wrong-doing, failed relationships, unachieved goals. I used to advise dying patients to do all they could to resolve these issues and I followed that advice myself when I neared death. I contacted many of the people I felt I had wronged or let down and apologized; they did not feel as antipathetic to me as I feared, so it helped to know I was not leaving too many scars behind. I also thanked people who I felt might feel taken for granted, and this was a rewarding experience although one of them called me a 'big Wally'.

All our lives contain regrets, moments of failure or badness, just as they do times of joy, kindness and success. For some reason as we die we worry about the bad things, the unresolved issues. This is even more difficult when the person we have regrets about is already dead; maybe we will meet them again – who knows? These can be very simple matters on the surface. For example a young man of thirty-five was dying of lymphoma (cancer of the lymph system). He was suffering greatly because he was surviving well beyond what had been expected by medical assessment. He seemed to be keeping himself alive by sheer will power and despite his endless suffering. Eventually he admitted he was fearful of dying because when he was fifteen he had stolen five pounds from his now dead mother at a moment when she was desperately short of money. He had never confessed this to her, never made the amends he always meant to do; he feared if he met her again on the other side, he would be ashamed and in trouble. What this implied about his mother's personality, his own relationship with her and his fear of her can only be conjectured. It was necessary to talk with him reassuringly and point out that the very fact he had felt the way he had and prolonged his suffering as a result, might be seen by any fair observer as enough punishment for such an error. He agreed to accept this – 'maybe so', he said; he observably relaxed and died two days later more at peace with himself.

Using the dying period when possible to relieve feelings and to resolve as many loose ends as you can is one way of making a positive use of the dying period, where the dying person feels this right for themselves. I know it helped me towards a less fearful acceptance of the inevitable.

I think now it is time to look at some of the contro-versial issues that surround death and dying, bearing in mind this background.

Disclosure

Not all dying people know from their doctors that they are dying. Doctors make a decision whether to disclose the fact or not, according to the circumstances of each case. The doctors may also be reluctant to admit they can no longer help and want to continue to try to do so against the odds.

Finding the appropriate time to tell someone when they are dying may also be a problem. The diagnosis may not be absolutely clear, it may be felt that telling the patient might significantly harm their health; neverthe-less modern practice is to accept that the patient has a right to know *if they ask*. It is surprising how reluctant you can feel actually to ask and how reluctant doctors are to give a very clear answer.

I eventually asked and was told that I should realize that my condition had worsened; it was time to be as-sessed for a transplant, and I should now think in months rather than years. Later, a doctor, giving me a second opinion, said it would be weeks rather than months and that my chances of getting a transplant in time were remote. Did my consultant respond to my fears of early death by offering a hope of a transplant? I cannot be sure; I hope not.

It seems to me a dying person has a right to know they are dying, what the process is likely to be, and how long it might take. Doctors need to complete the diagnostic process before they talk to the patient about it, but even if the process is incomplete in some way or uncertain in some aspects (such as length of time), the dying person should be told the situation. If the situation is not honestly disclosed, a web of deceit and false hope surrounds the dying person and their carers. This inhibits their chance to put their lives in what order they can and say the kind of goodbyes they want. It can also adversely affect palliation if treatments continue.

It can be argued that some people are too fragile or distressed to be able to handle such knowledge, or even that their primary carers are. Of course there may be exceptional cases where specific circumstances suggest non-disclosure, but generally I feel a robust view should be taken of a person's ability to cope with such knowledge, because it is the truth. I remember a very fragile and disturbed woman dying of cancer. The doctor and her family concluded, because of her mental state, it would be better for her not to know. Yet she did know, and she discharged herself from hospital because she wanted to die at home, colluding with the message of uncertainty about her death by observing, 'If I am going to die, I want to do it in my own bed'.

The failure to tell a dying person they are dying stands against what is their own growing internal awareness of dissolution. They need to share this awareness and not face repeated denials of its validity or prevarications about it from their medical carers.

Ending curative treatments

Given the implications, ending curative treatment is an admission that the dying process is irreversible in a particular case. Precisely when that position is reached is a difficult matter of judgement. In the case of the child dying of leukemia the odds of less than twenty per cent were taken by his parents, thus continuing treatment and affecting palliation and probably the length of the suffering. Ending treatment when even a faint chance of success exists is a difficult option. Our attitudes to health care are predisposed to a curative approach; palliation ought to prevent such action.

It may be we need to challenge some of these prevailing attitudes when it is clear the likelihood of death is greater than the chance of improvement. We need to do this from a compassionate point of view to lessen suffering and create acceptance. We may also be wise to do so from a resource point of view in as much as misdirected care is a bad use of scarce resources.

The dilemma will remain as to both the timing and wisdom of ending curative treatments in favour of improved palliation. I personally felt that holding out to me the possibility of transplant when it was clear I was unlikely to make it was unintentionally cruel. I would have preferred better management of my increasing symptoms and physical distress; however I have to be honest, when an outside chance of curative treatment came, I took it.

Exploitation

The physical dependence of dying people can make them vulnerable to exploitation. We all hear of cases where a dying person has felt to have been unduly influenced to change their will in someone's favour, often outside the family.

In one case a woman of sixty was dying. She also lived alone, her two children lived abroad. They had both visited her, and one invited her to join her in Hong Kong. She refused and told them not to worry; she wanted to die in her own home with her own things around her. She had always been a self-sufficient, unfussy woman content with her own company since her husband's death. She promised to ask her children to come at once when it was time. In the event her niece, who lived near, became a regular visitor as she neared her end and eventually moved in to help her. The woman became less assured as she faced death and was very dependent upon the care of her niece. She came to feel her own children did not care for her enough to be with her when she really needed them, but they felt the niece had disguised their mother's deteriorating condition and were surprised when she died. Whatever the rights and wrongs of the children, their mother changed her will and left half her estate and her London flat to her niece. It raises a question as to whether she was led into that act in a time of vulnerability.

As far as can be discovered the niece did not know about this change, though she took the benefit of it. However, the physical and psychological vulnerability of the dying raises questions for carers. Carers need to be sure they are not exploiting dying people either directly or covertly, or even unknowingly. We might need to bear two criteria in mind:

1. Is the dying person as comfortable and content as possible?

2. Am I able to act objectively for the dying person or am I myself in need of help?

Dying people will be vulnerable because of their own needs and because people may see an advantage to themselves in the situation. As a result criteria need to be in place to protect them from undue influence and other forms of exploitation, but not from themselves. Dying people like anyone else have the right to make decisions others may not approve of.

Euthanasia

The arguments for and against euthanasia are well rehearsed. On one hand the dying person has a right to die and avoid future suffering for themselves and others. On the other, it is necessary to be sure proper consent has been obtained and that the person understands that euthanasia may be a form of suicide, unacceptable to some on moral grounds.

I am personally reluctant to support euthanasia. First it does seem to me to be a form of suicide and I feel that, however difficult, we ought not to take such an option. Inconsistently, I have had pets put down when they were ill to avoid further suffering. Second it seems to me, given the vulnerability of the dying person, hard to be sure that the consent to death and the request it be assisted is entirely free of influence. This must be even more difficult when a person is in doubtful mental health and to some degree the objective judgement of the assisting person is involved.

Even in straightforward cases these issues emerge. No-one wants anyone to suffer prolonged symptoms such as pain and vomiting. If they choose not to suffer them, fair enough, some believe. I think fear is very much behind such an understandable attitude; fear of suffering, dependence and loss of control. What is the point of dealing with such things if the end is near. Part of this fear may be due to a lack of understanding that symptom control is or should be available. Dying people who do not choose euthanasia often find a time when their condition plateaus out and enables them to do meaningful things in preparation for their coming death. However, if we want to avoid a growing demand for euthanasia, we must make sure enough palliative care is available and the benefits of it understood.

I felt no desire myself for death as my symptoms varied; indeed I resented the fact I was dying while being afraid of increased discomfort and death itself. Euthanasia was to me irrelevant because to me suffering is something you have to go through as it is part of life itself. I thought others would help see that suffering was palliated as time passed. This meant I had enough confidence there would be limits to my suffering. Thus I was not tempted by suicide or euthanasia. I find it hard to separate the two, though I feel I should.

Nevertheless I can understand that there might be a point when death seems preferable to life and it could be a rational choice to choose to die. I once contemplated suicide myself many years ago and, once thought of as a way out, it was hard to let it go. In the end, I feel that euthanasia, where someone helps you die, is unacceptably dangerous as an option because of its openness to exploitation. Personal suicide, effected by yourself in private, I can understand and appreciate the reason for. Yet in the end something in me says that life, however bad, is all we have and we must endure even a harsh ending to it. I just hope I am able to bear the burden of that view if I come to death in pain and fear.

Do not resuscitate (DNR)

There is a widespread practice not to relieve, for example, with antibiotics, secondary illnesses that might affect the very old or terminally ill. The argument is that it is best to let nature take its course rather than intervene where the quality of life will continue to be poor. Some people particularly request this, as I did if I suffered a stroke or brain damage as a result of my operation. In cases where the person is senile or demented then, if they themselves left no indication, it needs to be decided by the relations and doctor in consultation.

Of course anxieties arise from this practice relative to whether the person's real wishes have been ascertained or could be reasonably surmised, or whether relatives' or doctors' anxiety to be free of the need to care have dominated the situation. This is a real concern and has to be guarded against.

I suppose this is partly a matter of the way you see things as regards the dying person in a terminal state. This is particularly acute as a problem in prolonged terminal conditions, advanced senility or vegetative state. In these cases, when no improvement is likely and no contribution can be made by the dying person, it might be compassionate to let them die when afflicted by something like pneumonia. It can also be argued that such persons, by ensuring resources are allocated to work of sheer compassion, are creating both jobs and the spirit of reverence for life; a spirit much needed in a savage world.

Conclusion

Life is a miracle, the odds on our existence at all were enormous. The survival of our life is thus very precious as you will be a long time dead. All the experiences of life, including suffering and its relief, compassion and pity, are important and there to be embraced. To me life is something to be celebrated and death something to be endured as part of the universal experience of entropy. I have no answers to the difficult questions surrounding death and dying. Yet I want to affirm the value of life in all its difficulties and in the face of suffering.

Chapter 6
The Patient
and the Clinical Trial

Participating in a clinical trial or in some medical research poses issues for the patient doing it and for those conducting the trial. Of course there are clear protocols that require that participants know why they are so participating and that participation cannot happen without their consent, and also that they know precisely what is being done. I hope, in the face of well publicized cases to the contrary, people do consent freely and know what they are consenting to.

Different perspectives

The first thing worth remembering is the different perspectives of the various parties to an experimental process. The doctors/researchers are trying to establish the basis for a new treatment, drug or procedure. The simple fact that they have got to the point of making a clinical trial, means that they have a vested interest in its success and can become involved in a less objective way; they want to succeed.

The 'guinea pigs' in the research, however, have other motivations. Of course they want the new process to be successful too; they want to be associated with success. Some may be entirely concerned with this as they will feel good about any altruistic results that may occur. Nevertheless they want to do this with minimum discomfort and careful monitoring and a way out with minimal consequences if things go awry. A few are participating because it is that or death, as happened to me. It is hard to contemplate that death might be a better option where suffering is great. For example, a man on renal dialysis described in an earlier chapter could be treated, but found the slow decline of his quality of life made it preferable to die and get it over with. A few participate for money, in effect earning a little for lending their bodies for non life-threatening research. Why not? They are selling their time as do all employees.

The view of research funders may also be different and varied. Commercial funders may feel enormous pressures to produce a return on research and development costs, and be inclined to down grade or ignore negative results. This is why these matters are carefully regulated. Charity and other funders also feel pressures

to succeed and show positive benefit resulting from donors' generosity or efforts; funders may, knowingly, or
not, exert strong pressures on researchers for positive results. Indeed research is often 'sold' in anticipation of
success.

The elements for conflict are clear in this area, but
the conflict is usually strangely subdued, half hidden
because of the mutual interest in success and the fact
that all are enthusiastic for safeguards and controls. As
one researcher revealingly told me, 'You have to go
through the hoops of getting approval and informing
the patients, rightly so, but then we can get on with
what really matters – the research'.

An interesting influence is the general public, some
section of whom may benefit from the research. I am
sure the public holds no one view but many, but they
certainly expect safety in experimentation. The rise and
passion of animal rights groups does not however seem
to have been paralleled by a similar movement con-
cerning clinical trials on humans; indeed, one MP, a sup-
porter of animal rights, told me as I lay recovering, that
human beings, 'Had to have the courage to experiment
on themselves rather than on helpless creatures'. He
meant it as a compliment, but the idea went down like a
lead balloon for two reasons. The first was that I was not
at the stage of recovery where I felt optimistic or painless. The second was because I knew two perfectly

healthy sheep had been given heart assist devices and that I was glad at least they had survived and were still munching away; their experience encouraged me to have a go.

So at the back of all research lies this vast amorphous and contradictory public concern. One researcher called it the sleeping dragon, but probably the media are its awakeners, being interested to find a story and exploit any controversial angle of it, or any heart warming angle. Should those sheep have gone through an operation so I could be safer? I do not know the answer to this, I feel so of course, and for anyone interested, Doris and Elsie have lived longer than most sheep!

Assessing

Not everyone can participate in a clinical trial. I expect this is a good thing on the whole, but there is a sense we all do in that we use prescription drugs or surgical procedures that were once part of clinical trial and are still monitored. We are the beneficiaries, or maybe ongoing participants by another facet of research monitoring.

In the sense meant here, however, access is voluntary, we must choose freely to participate in a clinical trial; given the complexities, this is sometimes no easy choice. I am going to use my own case to illustrate some of these dilemmas.

Having a titanium pump planted in the lower left ventricle of your heart to improve blood supply to the arteries is no small thing. The proposal to do it, reasons for it, and likely benefits are easy to grasp. It is less easy, unless you are a doctor, to understand the surgical process proposed, or the impact it will have on your body. In the absence of any clinical evidence, the likely aftercare was mostly guesswork, based on the experience of somewhat similar mitral valve replacement operations or quadruple bypasses. These are well reasoned expectations; after all the thoracotomy wound needed is not new, but not only are all cases a little different because of the individual involved, but the response of the body to the intrusion of a metal pump has to be considered. However some expectations of the time taken to recover can be too rigidly followed when the patient is doubtful about his or her capacity, and the doctors' expectations are influenced also by other factors such as cost and use of resources. The patient on the other hand needs what is needed.

I noticed on the Cardiothoracic Unit that there was an expectation to discharge the patient as soon as possible. This was because a patient can recover at home after a certain stage, but it is also imperative to have beds available for others needing the surgery. In the eleven weeks I was in hospital, quite a few patients felt unready to leave, but did not feel able to challenge the doctors about it, and sometimes even reassured them how much

I wanted to be home. I know that when I was discharged, I didn't feel ready, but felt I ought to go, so was to some extent pretending to agree with the doctors this was now right. The fact that I had twice to return for various periods seems to me to bear out my point.

To access experimental treatment is to have to cope with a larger measure of uncertainty as to the outcome than is usual. In non life-threatening cases this may not be too important as long as precautions are taken. In terminal cases the risk is of earlier death than might otherwise have been the case or enhanced suffering, as in chemotherapy trials, which existing weakness make it hard to endure.

Access can also be about rejection. You might not qualify for treatment or be strong enough for it. The necessary process of assessing people for heart transplantation is not just a lottery about who is around at the time, but is about who is best able to benefit. I know I was worried when I finally decided to try it because of my age, general condition and poor kidney function. This was a worry in accessing the Jarvik clinical trial as well; was I too far gone, as I felt I might be. To raise a hope you might live when you may already have passed some point of no return can be a cruel thing.

Access can be problematic. A choice has to be made by both you and those managing the experimental procedures, so there is an inevitable loss of power over their life by the patient. Not only must the patient be willing to have the experience, but so must the providers be willing to have you as a candidate. So it becomes, or could become, a classic case of patient rights against doctors' judgement. Certainly before my operation, when I was being managed by drugs and the only solution was a transplant, it seemed to me very hard to break through to even get assessed for a transplant; first I was too well, then possibly too sick. So you can feel a Catch 22.

I know the medical profession is keen to leave as much power as possible over decisions about their future to the patient. That must be right; the medical profession is there to serve the patient's need. The sheer disparity, however, between the patient's knowledge and physical weakness, and the skill and experience of professionals creates a dependence. Not all doctors are patient or skilled enough socially or psychologically to manage that situation. The fact that doctors *talk* a lot about patient self-determination, and the rights of patients to disclosure, is evidence of an imbalance in the relationship. This can make patients angry and irrational in their responses, thus compounding communication problems. So in assessing any experimental programme you are embracing possible conflicts like that. The unknowns are greater so experience is not a general guide and the patient has had to make an *a priori* judgement to trust those carrying out the research.

The overlook of hell

When treatment of an experimental kind begins you have to face up to three things:

1. The fact of the extent of your illness and the likely odds on success

2. The possibility of increased discomfort and suffering

3. The possibility of a negative outcome.

Sometimes it is hard to be exactly aware of how sick you are. The doctors may be loath to tell you or ambiguous about it. They told me, for example, I should plan on weeks not months, so, of course, I planned not at all, just hoped it would go away. The odds for my treatment were thought to be about fifty-fifty; good odds compared with some, but based only on the fact it had not been done with a view to permanence before. Being very sick, though, is something you don't really want to admit; I preferred death to creep up on me and hope it wouldn't be too uncomfortable. The Germans once had a political objective called the 'Drang nach Osten', the drive to the east to dispossess other inhabitants and provide room for themselves. I wondered why this idea always flashed into my mind when I thought about my getting more help. I needed a 'Drang nach Osten' to survive and of course that raised moral issues. Getting treatment through the use of scarce and precious resources with poor odds of success kind of disposes of those who might otherwise have used the resources. So in facing up to the imminence of death and turning to new means to survive, you might be parasitic upon rather than beneficial to the community.

If you are near death, you are having enough suffering. It is one thing to take medicine and procedures to reduce suffering, another to, with low odds of success, possibly increase your suffering. I suppose this thought and the questions as to whether you have had enough, or how influenced you are by others who want you to leave no stone unturned in the struggle to live informs your reactions to joining a trial.

I have noticed that there does come a point, sooner or later depending on the person, when you have had enough of suffering. You become less tolerant of the suffering you are experiencing, more demanding for relief and impatient with day-to-day matters. Thus to steel yourself for more suffering in your weakened circumstances is hard.

Finally, there is the possibility of failure and death. It is no good going into experimental treatment thinking it can only end positively. Of course a positive attitude helps and a will to live, but there also has to be some reconciliation with the potential to fail. In my case this was easy as I was near death, so what did it matter, but this is not always the case; sometimes people are far enough away from death for extra suffering to matter a lot. We also have the example of the man described earlier who abandoned long-time palliation of his renal condition when he felt the quality of his life had deteriorated enough.

I personally felt it was like walking along a narrow path at the edge of a great cliff from which you could easily fall into a hole. *Kyrie Eleison* I thought.

The shock of the new

There are three elements to the participation in an experimental treatment or research that need considering. The first is a public one, the interest in the new and what it might mean. The second, touched on before, is the individual's own fuller realization of how much their life was a benchmark for future work and so how much risk they took. The final aspect concerns the questions the new procedure raises in the field.

Any new procedure that brings radical new possibilities to the care or prevention of disease and illness is bound to attract public attention. The media are interested in demonstrating what has been done that is new and the human story behind it. The innovators are anxious to maintain funding for this work, to show the success of their endeavours and a new contribution to medical practice. The patient might like the public attention for a time, but essentially wants to get on, privately, with the life they have, or have had restored to them. These three perspectives are not necessarily compatible and one of the consequences of being involved in experimentation is the intrusion, welcome or not, of public interest in your life. The patient can become a kind of exhibit of the procedure or method, there to demonstrate the utility of the treatment and the human qualities of their life now preserved for a time. Such an experience is a shock. You don't fully anticipate it, but you are stuck with it. It is something you have to learn to cope with alongside your recovery.

The impact of public attention on the individual has, however, another more subtle effect. It illuminates to the patient the extent of the risk they may have taken as a sick or needy person and in becoming a kind of public property. On the one hand you are glad you made a contribution, on the other you are thinking how near you came to something worse. What is more, not everything in your life is good, so you can fear the discovery to a sometimes rapacious media of your faults. For me it was not only the overwhelming public interest that was a shock. I had expected some, but not the extent of it, but also the death of the second person, Jeff Coates, who received the pump during the same trial that disconcertingly illustrated my 'luck' in surviving. I am very glad further procedures have been successful.

First, public issues surround new treatments. In my case there are issues about how this will affect the treatment of cardiomyopathy and the future role of, or need for, transplants as the new treatment develops. In the United States the method is only used as a bridge to transplant. One wonders if, in many cases, it might replace the need for transplants for which organs are scarce. There is also a question of value for money. Experimental treatments impinge on resources needed for other things. The extent, therefore, to which they should have a call on health service budgets or be privately funded is important; it is a shock to realize you are a cost.

Examples abound of this, notably in infertility treatment where the trend has long been to provide the more radical treatments, such as IVF, privately rather than on the health service. Infertility is not life threatening and thus would not be important enough to attract substantial public funding in a time of public concern about it as a problem. Terminal illness also raises such questions; on the one hand everyone wants to relieve suffering, on the other, what is the value of continuing curative treatments when the odds of success are very low (less than fifty per cent say). Behind these considerations is a suffering person often helpless to defend their rights.

Filthy lucre

For all our pride in the Health Service, it costs. Care is a commodity like most things involving choice as to what to and what not to fund. The costs of established care are high and the resources (human and financial) insufficient to cover the need, thus research into new procedures and methodology is hard to justify except on a cost-saving basis.

Nevertheless improved treatments, better care and better understanding of causes and effects are necessary to a dynamic health service. Government policy seems to be to encourage experimentation in the private and charitable sectors rather than from mainstream funds. Nevertheless there are areas of dispute and cover-up. Let me illustrate this from my own experience. My operation and hospital costs were paid for by The National Heart Research Fund and The Artificial Heart Fund. Technically this should mean no costs or resource implications exist for health service funds. Not so; extra resources in intensive care were only available from existing provision and thus other operations were delayed; moreover, after discharge, a dispute arose about paying for normal ongoing outpatient maintenance. The John Radcliffe Hospital continued to charge The Artificial Heart Fund for this unless they could get it funded by The Birmingham Health Authority where I live. This is absurd; ongoing supervision needs to be routinely provided by the team who developed the treatment and not be a burden on a Fund paying for further treatment. Patients should have the right to have this ongoing care at the place of original treatment where there is real knowledge and experience of the situation. Sometimes you feel, as a patient, just a pawn in a funding game.

Some attention needs to be given to the boundaries in experimental care as to where private funding stops and public funding begins, so patients and charities do not lose out in jurisdictional disputes.

Of course humankind invented money and it cannot be uninvented in favour of a system based on need. It is an astonishing fact of human history that something so nebulous and trust-based as money has such a hold on modern society. We have made money a commodity although it doesn't really exist. It is because of this that health care is a commodity subject to the laws of supply and demand, particularly as regards the value of money. In these circumstances the leavening of purely supply and demand aspects of health in favour of human need is essential; maybe health care policy is about getting that balance as right as it can be at any given time.

De profundis

In another chapter I looked at the kind of questions dying people ask about life, its meaning and its future, if any, after death. In some senses it is not surprising that people who are facing the possibility or certainty of death should ask such questions; on the other it aligns such debates alongside suffering and dissolution. Dying is a very emotional experience with sharp mood swings and an intense need for affection and care. It helps when the dying person's questions about the meaning of life or the future are listened to and responded to as best can be done.

Of course, whether God exists or not, or whether God is good in ways we see as good are really unanswerable questions. People do not have the knowledge or experience to answer them, or the perspective God must have if he or she or it exists. Sometimes people have experiences that lead them either to maintain the existence of God or develop faith in a particular view or perspective of God such as Catholicism or Islam. It is doubt, however, that seems to me to be the hallmark of the present age. Faith is in retreat, although of course those with faith would argue differently. The prospect of death raises the questions and doubts in stark way, with sometimes bitter undertones. I think most dying people think hard about this at some point as do many carers watching death. I know I think about such matters more than most, as I have a kind of angst about 'Dasein' as Heidegger called Being. Nevertheless, others who were dying thought about such things too, so maybe I was not so unusual.

I think most dying people, although I don't think this is true of their carers, reach some kind of answer about the deeper questions. My view went like this:

1. I exist but will soon cease to exist.

2. I am not sure one can know why I existed, let alone why humankind does.

3. Nevertheless the fact that I did exist must have some consequences or even meaning.

4. It is no good considering religious responses to such matters, as actually they may not answer the question with any indisputable certainty.

5. A pond is changed by a ripple for two reasons. For example the pond is altered by what is causing the ripple, a stone thrown in for example, or a duck diving to eat some pond life. The surface is also changed temporarily by the impact of the event. Thus by the very act of existing, something, however small or transitory has been changed permanently by our life. We thus contribute to the development of the universe.

6. I do not know whether life, in some way, continues after death, though I would like to feel it did.

7. Religion teaches the certainty it does, at least mine does.

8. Therefore I will rely on that experience knowing it may be an act of the human imagination. This reliance reaches deep into myself.

9. Therefore I feel connected in some way to the universe that is about to devour me.

This is what death drew me near to as a dying person. Strangely it is to do with affirming life in the face of dissolution. It is in the end an interior experience, but a source of courage even if it is a resolute belief not to believe. Thus death for all its grimness is also an affirmation of the self and of life. Thus to win through is to be life-affirmed.

Trivia

I think it is wise not to omit the trivial things that occur in the experience we have both as a dying person and as someone taking a risk in a clinical trial. The small things tell me a lot.

Was there a point, I asked the anaesthetist, casually one day, months after the operation, when you thought you might lose me? 'It was touch and go when we couldn't stop the bleeding', he said, 'You needed a huge amount of blood, but once you were successfully extubated, we knew you would be all right'. Extubation took place on the fourth day after the operation. This statement was a confirmation to me of the risk I had taken. I felt gratitude to all those anonymous blood donors whose donations had bought me my life.

Hospital food was another problem. When you have a poor appetite and are a bit low, the advent of reconstituted and reheated food makes you mad. It is a sign of disrespect for the patient, or a serious English masochism about food that allows such poor quality fare be served at all. You realize it is all a matter of cost; only those not eating the food on a day-to-day basis could imagine that the cheapest food on the most basic of menus is adequate. People in charge of hospital food should be required to eat it; I never met one who did more than sample it.

'Could you just clean the floor', I asked a nursing auxiliary, as my wife was due and it was a bit tatty. 'I'll see if I can find the cleaner', she said, disappearing with haste and not reappearing. In some pain and exhaustion I bent down and picked the mess up, piece by piece, and then got told off by the nurse for doing it and told to wash my hands. I didn't find the hospital dirty, but it wasn't really clean either. The cleaners looked bored and were sometimes slapdash, but maintained a minimal standard. I spilt a drink once in the middle of the night, and the nursing auxiliary who cleaned it up asked me if I was glad she had to strain her back because of my clumsiness. I told her I was; she was furious, patients are supposed to be passive and not troublemakers.

A woman in the bed opposite was in the early stages of senile dementia. She was sometimes violent with the nurses, but they never held it against her, feeling pity for her even when she hit them. This illustrated the professionalism of the nurses and their calm in the face of difficulty. After weeks in hospital, with few exceptions, I learned to have great respect for them.

I was in a supermarket, probably only the second time since I came out of hospital; it used to be quite an expedition to go. On this day a large lady asked me what was that thing in my head. I explained; she had a close look. 'Come and see this', she said to her two kids, 'it is marvellous what they can do today'.

'You can't be in as much pain as this', a doctor told me; 'you better believe it', I replied. I am not at all sure he did. Doctors seem to me to get fixed ideas of how you are progressing and dislike any indications to the contrary. It must be psychological, I was told. Get a bloody psychologist then, I said, but of course they didn't. It will all pass said the Consultant, implying there was no need to do much and trying to reinforce my self-confidence. I wish you would pass away I thought.

'How are you feeling?' my GP asked, just after my discharge. She meant it well and nothing deep, but my goodness, what a question. How can you explain the fear, the pain, the elation, the weariness, the exuberant expectation of life. 'OK', I said, 'better than before'. She smiled, had a listen to my pump and took some blood samples. She was an understanding GP in my view, but that question was disconcerting.

I met the wife of Robert Jarvik the inventor of the heart pump I use. She is a famous personality in her own right, Marilyn Vos Savant the advice columnist for *Parade* magazine in the United States. She is said to have one of the highest IQs in the world. Her seven sacred virtues which she set out in the December 5th, 2000 issue of *Parade* magazine are inspiring and came to set out some of the bases upon which I want to build my new life. I think they contain the call to tolerance and understanding the modern world so much needs. They deserve consideration – here they are:

1. The Humility to know that we are not alone in the world.

2. The Generosity to allow others to have what they deserve.

3. The Restraint to control our most passionate impulses.

4. The Kindness to tolerate the mistakes of our fellow man.

5. The Moderation to satisfy ourselves with the necessities.

6. The Charity to help those who are unable to help themselves.

7. The Diligence to make ourselves useful in the modernworld.

Meeting new people, sharing who they are, being accepted, this is a new wonder of my life.

Dasein

I am a person, something unique, and yet I am just biologically a human male. I have the needs of a human being, yet I am also something different. I think this tension between our uniqueness and humanity exists in all of us.

Participating in a clinical trial made this point strongly to me. It was my physiology that was being treated, the human genetic inheritance. Doctors and nurses, whose job it is to improve those parts of that inheritance that are in trouble, are treating the physical part of me; of course they know my morals and feelings are important and try to accommodate them, but essentially I was experimental meat, a bit of live animal research.

The curious thing was the more I needed them and conformed to their physical advice, the more in my social self I wanted my right to be unique. Other patients often talked about how they hid their real feelings, anxious to get out of hospital to a kind of new freedom. It was sort of expected; one conformed. The difficult patients were those that didn't. Nevertheless, something changes within that asserts the self that says who we are. Bernard Alexander, the third person to have the operation I had, told me, as he recovered, he was going to sell his caravan site. What he wanted was to spend as much time with Val, his wife, as possible. This he had discovered was what mattered and was life affirming to him; I was touched, love was at the heart of who he was. I hope Val felt the same.

Dave Rutledge told me, as he recovered from appalling side effects following his heart surgery, that he just wanted to get back to normal and enjoy his hobby again, which was steam trains and hurdy gurdies. He was a man of sorrows, who had lost his only and beloved son in a car accident, but he still found joy in life in its simple things; I admired him. He was sympathetic and caring when I was down and he shared his own dependency too. The man knew how to be a friend.

Sitting in the hospital chapel during a Mass, still in a wheelchair, still in pain, still exhausted and uncertain I would ever fully recover, the Priest called, 'Lift up your Hearts', and we replied, 'We lift them up unto the Lord' in that mystic affirmation of the victory of life in the face of death. I cannot ever explain how grateful I am for the experience I had between life and death and then of a kind of resurrection. It has taught me I am and that I am glad that I am.

Chapter 7
Wider Implications and the Future

A growing number of people are alive because of the use of medical technologies. Perhaps the best known examples are dialysis patients who rely on what is in effect an artificial kidney. There are many others, people with colostomy bags, pacemakers, and so on. We are using mechanical means to replace or support the human physiology. Of course this is a great thing as it can prolong life and improve its quality, although in a few cases people have found the burden too great and chosen to die.

I sit here with my mechanical heart pump and wonder about death. Let me explain why. In an article in the *Sunday Times Colour Supplement* on 25th March 2001 Lois Rogers in describing my operation noted from her interview with the surgical team that, 'As he was regaining consciousness the day after the operation, he went into kidney failure. Miraculously, the supply of oxygenated blood provided by the pump restored the function.' The failure of one organ was corrected by the improvement to another by mechanical means. She goes on to say later, 'Even worse is the question of when a dead person with a heart pump should be switched off, and who should do it'.

This dilemma has already arisen. The second person to receive the pump, 58-year-old Jeffrey Coates, survived three months but it became clear the pump was not able to help because blood passing through his lungs was not becoming adequately oxygenated. This meant that in effect he was dead but for the pump. The surgeon and the family had to decide to turn it off so he could die.

I get to thinking, what would happen to me if I got old and unable to make decisions for myself; who will take the decision to turn my pump off and let me die? I suppose while I am *compos mentis* I can in theory do it myself, though I would find it difficult, as I would, if I were rational enough, wonder if I was committing suicide. I would want to die if I lost my faculties and lived only like a vegetable. If a population of people with heart pumps develops then they will have special needs and one of these may have to be to work out the circumstances in which their pump can be turned off.

In the past death always came to *us* and our society and thinking are, as a result, geared to that. Medical care has been organized to maintain life, and defeat disease and manage chronic conditions. Religious thought dealt with the physical ending that is death by providing some explanation of a post-death existence What happens if by organ support, replacement or repair, or the new nano-technologies we are able, except for accidents, to prolong life indefinitely?

Just a glance at the issues this would raise is disturbing. A huge increase in the older elderly population, an increase in the productive years, a dependence on medicine which would increase the influence of its practitioners not to mention its costs; the question of the ethics of death would have to be looked at again. For example, what would the attitude of say the Catholic church be to a member having to choose to die?

Medicine, as it has become more sophisticated and technological, has been increasingly concerned not only with recovery but also with ensuring 'quality of life'. What is the quality of life that makes life valuable rather than a matter of endurance? I am not myself, and never will be, as well as I was, but I am well enough to find life worthwhile despite the limitations. What will I do if I feel this is no longer the case?

I remember asking, just after the operation, whether I was alive. I started to explain what I meant to the young surgeon, Pedro Catarino for whose honesty and no nonsense approach I have great respect. Pedro knew what I meant and at once explained. If I meant was my heart functioning by itself as well as with the pump, then yes, I was alive. If I meant did I think I could survive without the pump, not at present, though the heart might heal over time. That was fair enough for me then. I wasn't dead, my own heart was functioning and there was a reasonable hope it would improve and with it my quality of life.

I did not know at that time how near I had been to death. According to the lead surgeon, Steve Westaby, 'Houghton died several times on the operating table. His liver was failing and could not pick up enough blood clotting factors. Then his heart packed up. We had to put him on a heart-lung machine, which is itself dangerous, much earlier than we intended to. We had enormous difficulty just keeping him alive. We couldn't stop him bleeding and his condition was getting worse and worse while we were trying to do this operation that had never been done before.' Should I be dead, I wondered, reading this later?

My very survival and present health demonstrate what was achieved by this dangerous experiment. Now other patients are surviving the operation and one hopes that an effective treatment for cardiomyopathy is emerging. As the population of survivors grows, so will the need to recognize them as a special group with specific needs and issues. I want to take a look at these issues.

Extra life

It surprises some people that I feel that 'extra life' is different in some ways from what we might call 'normal life'. I do not mean by this the problem of living holding a battery pack – though that is different. I haven't tried swimming yet!

I was thinking about the quality and maybe the feel of life. It does not seem so easy for me, or the three people successfully treated after me, or for people benefiting from other treatments that require external support, for example renal dialysis patients, people required to wear colostomy bags long term, people with pacemakers. I know because I have asked some of them and considered their insights in the light of how I feel myself.

What is different then? I think it might be best to think of this in three separate contexts. These are the context of monitoring and improving the quality of life, the context of independence and finally the less defined but important context of existential experience of life.

Quality of life

As regards the quality of life, it is of no use just to be alive, or just to hold at bay the dying process. To be valuable to the individual and to society, extra life has to enable the person to live with some prospect of personal growth and development and without fear of imminent death, pain or physical debility.

I have cared for renal dialysis patients who felt, after some years on the treatment, they wished to end it, and thus die. In their view the very slow decline in their standard of life, in their physical wellness, proved wearisome. This is not unknown among renal patients. It suggests to me that long-term benefit may be as important as short-term in assessing the value of extra life. In learning to live with limitations, they must not be such as to wear you away. One feature of my own condition is easy exhaustion, another the inability to go to work full time. I am sixty-two so it may not matter much, but it would if I were forty.

It is hard to be exact about what one means by quality of life. Almost any definition has its limitations. That life is relatively pain and symptom free is important; the ability to enjoy yourself and to travel seems necessary. You need something useful to do without it exhausting you. These are very simple things, but do illustrate what is meant by quality of life. One friend I talked to who has recently undergone surgery for cancer said that she felt she was on the mend when she was able to laugh again at predicaments other than her own. I think suffering can make you lose your sense of humour, so having a sense of humour becomes important, too, as it is a sign of wellness.

This leads to the second context – independence. People with extra life are not independent. At present they rely on continuing medical supervision and medical support. Someone, for example, has to make and service my batteries, or maintain a renal dialysis machine. We rely on a civilized society committed to keeping us going despite resource limits in health care.

Independence

Independence as an individual is something we take for granted. It is what we spent our childhood learning. Illness makes us dependent, so recovery needs to return us to independence. A number of factors define independence.

A first element must be to be mostly autonomous physically – to be able to walk, travel, feed yourself, toilet and prepare your own food or do your own chores. In doing that we are autonomous adults able to live in society. Loss of independence changes the basis of relationships, we become unequal, requiring society's charity rather than being a full participant. So independence depends on a good level of wellness.

It is important also to be independent financially: able to work, to earn enough at least to maintain your quality of life even if with social welfare income. I get what is called Severe Disablement Allowance from the UK government to help me and it does bridge the gap between my annuity, what I can earn and what I need. This means dependence on the social goodwill of our fellow citizens. In these circumstances it is important to be able to make some kind of valued return, to feel you are an asset to society not a burden. Money is the single most important element in enabling a quality of life; independence requires we have enough.

Existential experience

Finally there is the existential context of extra life. It is as if our earlier life has passed away forever; that is the unenhanced life that was our birth heritage and our experience. Someone once wrote 'the past is a foreign country' and that seems all too true. The proximity and imminence of death leaves its mark on your worldview (Weltanschauung). A characteristic of my own experience and that of others I have met in a similar position is a change of priorities. What is important ceases to be the human questions of family, career, interests, social relationships and becomes something else. Love is important, you appreciate love more. I feel a kinship with life I never felt before; it has become real to me in a new way.

It is like walking into Eden or reverting to the wonder of childhood.

There was a general election in the UK recently. Of course I voted, probably for Mr. Blair, but the election was less real for me in terms of its issues. I want to say, well what is government for and where are we going, not to distinguish between different scenarios for progress on education, health, and so on. I have become interested in fundamentals, as I never was before.

The big question, however, is what to do with this extra life. Years ago, when I was a young man, I suffered a bereavement. I was in South Africa, I felt I needed to be alone a while, so I went up to a farm near what is now the Namibian border, along the Orange river, and took a horse, pack horse and dog and just rode into the bushveldt. As I wandered around I encountered two of the Khoisan or Bushmen people – an old man and his grandson. We shared a fire and food together one memorable night. I was in a mood to do the then unthinkable, in Apartheid South Africa – spend a night as an equal, even as a student, with black citizens.

We sat beneath a Baobab tree watching one of those sudden African sunsets and talked in broken English and a little Afrikaans. The old man saw I was grieving and I just cried. He put out his old arm on to my knee and said words to this effect. 'My son, mantis takes her prey. Whoever falls into the jaws of mantis is lost ever,

147

part of mantis not himself. It is the way of things. Grief is saying goodbye but now my son ask this question only, what is the gift of mantis, for mantis does not take without return. What can I now do that hitherto I could not have done, for everything is renewed but not the same.'

This is my existential task: renewal in a new context of my life. For life is a gift to be used, not merely enjoyed – both between yourself and those you love and who love you, and in general.

A call to action

It feels odd, in your early sixties, to find yourself, however accidentally, someone whose experience is demonstrating not only a new way of dealing with terminal heart disease, but also someone facing the early manifestation of what may be a new culture of death and dying. I am not able to do more than flag up the problem, but I do this well in advance of it becoming a wider issue. We might, however, gain a lot from an overview of existing situations and of likely advances in medical practice where external artificial support is being provided or studied for people. An Extra Life Group devoted to this might consist not only of the medical pioneers and practitioners providing the services or possibilities, but their patients, who experience the consequences; ethical and moral thinkers and concerned lay persons; the relevant government departments; and medical, social and religious institutions and associations. Its first aim should be to get a picture of the existing and prospective extent of change and to devise some ways to think of the consequences on both society and individuals.

As a society, we also need to do something to ensure that the social and psychological effects of such procedures are better handled for the individuals concerned and for their relatives and friends. We need as a community, to look far more seriously at how to deal with the new phenomenon of life prolongation by mechanical means. We need the psychologists, therapists and social workers to become familiar with this issue.

Funding

It is clear to me that the whole question of funding experimental medicine needs to be examined, notwithstanding the strain of funding day-to-day medical services at good levels of resourcing. Medical research can save money, as it would in this case if the heart pump became widely used; but it also often makes unexpected changes in what is needed. For example, we need better psychological support, more specifically trained nurses and so forth. General practioners need support to provide ongoing help to mechanically assisted patients.

The right to die

There is one question that concerns me quite a lot. When is it right to die? The Inuit, in former times, when they were old or unable to do their part in their communities, would be left alone to die; their time was over. We may have to re-examine such matters. There are not unlimited resources and life without purpose can be seen as pointless. Who would or could decide such a matter except the sufferer? This might be the most frightening question in view of genocidal experience revolving around the rights of one group as opposed to another, for example in Nazi Germany.

Suppose we all live on to about 150. It is hard to imagine sharing the world with the fourth generation of your descendants, maybe even the fifth. Will we have fulfilled all our ambitions, done all we could do? Might we not be bored, might our quality of life be limited by tedium? We may need to have the right to die.

This raises questions about our reactions to death. The life force within us seems to demand fulfillment; death is defeat, ending or, if you adhere to some belief, transition to a new if uncontactable existence. I don't know what to say about death. I chose to try to live and, although I am a Catholic, I have no idea if there is life after death. Visions of hell and torment are none too attractive and heaven sounds a bit dull. Yet I feel that because biologically we are transient creatures, death is our destiny. Maybe we should be more accepting of it as we gain control of the physical factors that prolong life? This will mean that we will have to think about the question as to when death is the right thing for an individual.

It is not easy for me to think about such things. To me all life, however wounded, seems precious, needed and a miracle. I am appalled by loss of life and especially by loss of life imposed on one group or person by another. I would, for example, never be able to support the death penalty; and the horrors of Hitler's and Stalin's genocides and the many others since, trouble me. Yet I feel that we may have to try and find out when it is right to die and who should decide it, under what ethical and safety considerations.

Endings

'Peter', the nurse, Des Robson, on the surgical team, said to me recently, 'You think too much, you always worry about the most pessimistic rather than the most optimistic possibilities.' Well I am sure she is right, she had to put up with all my doubts and fears as I recovered, she deserves a medal just for that! So maybe I am a bit too dramatic.

I, of course, don't think so – and out of my own trauma and experience, I want to say to everyone,

'Come on guys, what are we doing? Thanks, of course, for doing it!'

Patient Care

The Physician's Role

Adrian Banning

Living with heart failure

Heart failure is a debilitating condition that has received little public attention. It is a syndrome that varies in intensity from a mild condition for which the patient takes medication but really has few symptoms, to a severe debilitating syndrome which persists despite multiple medications. In this fulminant form the patient can barely move without breathlessness and his or her life expectancy is worse than that of a patient with malignant cancers.

Increasing shortness of breath with exertion is the usual initial symptom of heart failure but this is rarely the only problem. Other common symptoms include malaise, fatigue and marked ankle swelling related to retention of fluid. When symptoms are poorly controlled, breathlessness may be particularly marked at night when the patient attempts to lie down to sleep. This sensation is often compared to that of drowning and patients will often resort to sleeping upright in their armchairs in order to get some rest.

One of the great frustrations of living with heart failure is that symptoms tend to vary from day to day. Sometimes symptoms are relatively minor and exercise can be undertaken with few restrictions. The next day symptoms may be crippling and even walking across the room can result in absolute exhaustion. This variability in symptoms and its lack of predictability has an inevitable effect on the patient's morale. Difficulty with exercise limits social contact considerably and this can result in isolation and depression.

In the last ten years a number of drugs have been proven to improve the expected lifespan of patients with heart failure. These drugs include angiotensin converting enzyme inhibitors, beta blockers and vasodilators. Unfortunately these drugs do not cure heart failure, but they do help the heart function more effectively with less risk of deterioration. Despite these drugs many patients remain breathless on exercise and need to take diuretic medications to reduce breathlessness, avoid fluid accumulation and swelling of the ankles. These drugs increase the amount of urine passed and reduce fluid retention. Their effect is powerful and almost immediate which results in a requirement to remain close to a lavatory for up to four hours. Inevitably, when taking these medications, patients become reluctant to leave their immediate surroundings without planning an escape route to a convenient lavatory and this accentuates social isolation. High doses of these diuretic drugs also cause their own problems inlcuding severe gout, which can be very difficult to treat effectively because of potential interactions between drugs.

The general objective of doctors treating heart failure is to prolong life, prevent deterioration and try and reduce symptoms. Complete cure is rarely possible but, with drugs, improved function of the heart will reduce perceived symptoms. Unfortunately for a minority, despite medication, symptoms are progressive and it is in this patient group that heart transplantation is considered. When heart transplantation is not possible because of a lack of availability of organs conventional medicine has little to offer apart from increasing doses of diuretics and it is in this group of severely ill patients that experimental therapies have been used.

Selecting patients for experimental therapies

Selection of patients for experimental treatments is extremely demanding for the doctor. There are enormous ethical and logistic issues which must be completely addressed initially, but even when this is done and a trial is ready to begin, the investigator must think quite carefully about how he is going to instigate recruitment of patients into a study. When the study involves life-threatening surgery this is particularly challenging. To obtain informed consent a frank and often blunt description of the patient's position must be offered. This assessment of the future with conventional therapy can then be put in context of the speculation surrounding the experimental therapy. It is crucial that the patient understands the risk they are taking and the inevitable uncertainty that this entails. For the investigator to be in a position to offer this new treatment they must ensure that all other potential conventional therapies have been exhausted.

In Peter Houghton's case, although this device had been implanted temporarily, no-one had ever had this device in the long term and the number of human implants was tiny. One had to ensure that Peter's enthusiasm to have surgery was tempered by a realization of a highly uncertain future. I drew the analogy to jumping from a diving board and not being sure whether there was any water in the pool below. The aim of the device was to improve quality of life; there were no guarantees at all about quantity of life. We hoped that if surgery was successful the need for diuretics would be reduced, as there would be less fluid retention, and that breathlessness would be significantly improved. Put succinctly, to obtain a better quality of life, Peter needed to gamble

his remainng life with severe symptoms against the risk
of dying in surgery.

Recovery

Once physical recovery is complete and the wounds
have healed there is an inevitable psychological price to
be paid for the process that a patient like Peter has undergone. To face death and to accept the risk of death,
but then to cheat death must inevitably alter one's per-
ception of life.

In Peter's case immediately after surgery the emphasis was on tomorrow and improved physical condition. However as time passed and the recovery continued, planning for next week began and then daring
to plan for next month. Recently plans have been made
for next year and beyond. Living with the uncertainties
of one's health and daring to enjoy one's improved
health are important issues. If you are the first patient
undergoing a study like this you are an icebreaker, you
are tackling new barriers and pushing back preconcep-
tions. I hope Peter can dare to resume a normal life with
almost normal expectations of quality of life. It is hoped
that these expectations will build and that his lifestyle
will continue to improve as he dares to live to the full
and enjoy the benefits of surgery. This challenge is perhaps as great as many of the others that he has already
faced and conquered.

Appendix 2

The Operation

Steve Westaby

After eight years of intensive laboratory research both in Oxford and the Texas Heart Institute we were ready for the first human implant. Both the Medical Devices Agency and the Ethics Committee in Oxford approved a limited clinical trial of the Jarvik 2000 Heart for patients with end stage cardiomyopathy who were ineligible for transplantation or not prepared to accept this option. The Oxford Team then endeavoured to recruit such patients.

Peter Houghton's referral was by a circuitous and unusual route. Dr Rob George at the Middlesex Hospital had been a colleague of mine many years ago and recalled articles about the Jarvik 2000 Heart by Lois Rogers in the Sunday Times. Rob was aware that Peter was very close to death from heart failure. Even with maximum drug treatment Peter could walk no more than 10 yards without exhaustion and breathlessness. His legs and abdomen were full of heart failure fluid. His kidney function was too poor to accommodate anti-rejection drugs in the event of consideration for a heart transplant. In a last ditch effort to intervene on Peter's behalf Rob George contacted me in Oxford and outlined the problem. He emphasized that Peter was an extremely intelligent man with insight into his own fate but felt that he would be prepared to take the chance of life with the new device. I responded by suggesting that Peter should come to Oxford as soon as possible so that we could assess him.

Two days later I met Peter in my office. He had a broad grin but was too breathless to get up after coming from the car-park in a wheel-chair. It was immediately apparent that Peter had a lively brain in a body completely devastated by terminal heart failure. There was little doubt that Peter would fulfil the criteria for the clinical trial. My main concern was that he had reached the stage where he might not survive the operation. The Jarvik 2000 Heart takes over the function of the left ventricle but it was clear that Peter also had advanced right ventricular failure.

After discussing the potential risks and benefits of the implant, Peter left to consider his options whilst we decided on a schedule of tests to confirm his suitability. Cardiac catheterization showed no evidence of coronary artery disease but a worrying degree of pulmonary hypertension and right heart failure. Kidney function was also significantly depressed.

In the mean time Professor Bud Frazier in Houston and Robert Jarvik in New York were alerted to the potential date of June 20th 2000 for the first permanent implant of the Jarvik 2000 Heart. This was the second alert. The first potential patient, a 31-year-old female had been claimed by a transplant team and died without treatment.

Professor Phillip Poole-Wilson of the Royal Brompton Hospital was asked to review and confirm Peter's status as our first candidate. We provisionally admitted Peter to the John Radcliffe Hospital a week before the implant to intensify his medical treatment. Poole-Wilson returned from an international conference at 9.00pm the same day and took a taxi from Heathrow to Oxford to assess Peter. He arrived at 10.00pm and spent ninety minutes in private conversation after which Peter was deemed the ideal candidate.

Poole-Wilson left Oxford at 11.30pm to return home to South London whilst we contacted Dr Jarvik and Bud Frazier with an affirmative answer.

The Team assembled in Oxford on the evening before surgery and Peter was brought to the intensive care unit for advanced preparation. Arterial, venous and pulmonary arterial catheters were inserted for monitoring overnight. The drug Milrinone was infused to reduce the pressure in the right heart and lungs. A deeply religious man, Peter was calm throughout and quite prepared for both potential outcomes. In the mean time the team met to finalize the surgical strategy and contingency plans for the potential complications.

On the morning of the 20th there was considerable excitement and a degree of apprehension at the Hospital. Westaby met with Frazier for breakfast at the Randolph Hotel then went on to Operating Theatre 5 and first closed a hole in the heart of a three-month-old baby. As this procedure was going on Peter underwent the final preparations including shaving the surgical sites on the left side of the head, the neck, the chest and the groin. As the baby left the operating theatre Peter was finally anaesthetized, the point of no return. Predictably there were problems almost immediately with low blood pressure and right heart failure. Very sick patients do not easily tolerate being tipped into the lateral position required to perform the operation. Intravenous drugs improved the situation and he was brought through to the operating theatre soon after the baby left.

The Theatre suite was already crowded with the surgical team and hopeful spectators. In an attempt to minimize the numbers in the operating room we had already arranged to relay the procedure by camera to a Lecture Theatre. Even the positioning of Peter on the operating table proved difficult. He weighed 115kgs and the skin over his edematous legs and sacrum broke easily. Great care was taken to cushion these areas from potential trauma or pressure sores. In addition we had to expose the left side of the neck and head in order to implant the innovative skull-mounted pedestal system for the power supply. This was the first time that this approach had ever been used and we had asked Mr Andrew Freeland (an experienced ear, nose and throat surgeon) to help with this. Freeland had considerable experience of cochlear implants for deafness and the skull-mounted power system was based on this technology.

Peter was comprehensively painted with the iodine skin preparation then covered in paper drapes leaving the surgical sites exposed. The skin was dried and covered with adhesive plastic drapes. In the mean time the technicians prepared the heart lung machine and Dr Jarvik began to unpack the components of the Jarvik 2000 Heart. This is a remarkable thumb-sized titanium axial flow pump with a fabric graft which re-routes the blood from inside the left heart to the major artery, the aorta. The Jarvik 2000 Heart was implanted into Peter's own failing heart to take over the function of the left pumping chamber. Two teams worked on the three separate surgical sites. Andrew Freeland was assisted by my surgical Fellow, Pedro Catarino, whilst I opened the chest assisted by Satoshi Sato from Tokyo. Bud Frazier joined us to implant the pump.

The first step was to open the left side of the chest through the bed of the sixth rib thereby exposing the heart and the descending thoracic aorta. The Jarvik 2000 Heart and power system were then brought into the surgical field in order to convey the cable from the apex of the chest through the neck and to a site on the skull about 10 cms behind the ear. Peter had poor liver function and had received long-term warfarin therapy. This resulted in substantial bleeding from all the surgical sites.

With the chest open I made four incisions in the neck to convey the power cable in zig-zag fashion to the site on the skull prepared by Andrew Freeland. Andrew had drilled six small holes into the outer table of the skull through which the screws which secured the titanium pedestal would be passed. Using a blunt dissecting forcep I produced a tunnel from the shoulder incision into the apex of the left chest and withdrew the power cable to the neck. Repeating this process through the different surgical incisions I delivered the three-point connector to the skull pedestal and Andrew screwed this to the skull.

By this time the anaesthetist, David Piggott, was concerned about Peter's heart function. The blood pressure had fallen to less than 60 mm Hg and the pressure in his pulmonary artery now exceeded the systemic pressure. Cardiac arrest was imminent so I shifted my attention to the third surgical site in the groin in order to cannulate the blood vessels to the leg and join Peter to the Heart-Lung machine. I cannulated the femoral artery first and then passed a long thin walled cannula from the femoral vein into the right-sided collecting chamber of the heart. We needed to prevent clotting altogether with heparin before beginning cardio-pulmonary bypass and this added further to the bleeding tendency. Bud Frazier joined me at this point. We decided with David Piggott that we could not wait any longer without the heart-lung machine and we therefore started cardio-pulmonary bypass.

At the same time an audience including many of the heart surgery trainees and nurses had assembled in the Lecture Theatre to watch the procedure on the video link. As Peter's condition deteriorated I asked for the sound to be switched off. It is not always easy to remain polite in these circumstances.

Once Peter was on the heart lung machine he was safe and we did not have to rush the rest of the procedure. Andrew Freeland closed the wounds on the head and shoulder. Dr Jarvik attached the external power system consisting of a controller and lithium battery both about the size of a portable telephone. At the same time I applied a side clamp to Peter's aorta and joined a

16mm vascular graft to it with a continuous stitch. When I released the side clamp I was concerned that the aorta itself was fragile. I reinforced part of the suture line with teflon buttressed stitches. We then turned our attention to the most important and exciting part of the procedure, implantation of the Jarvik 2000 Heart inside Peter's own left ventricle.

The Jarvik 2000 is held in place by a sewing cuff sewn on to the apex of the left ventricle. We used large stitches with teflon buttress to prevent them pulling through the fragile muscle. When the cuff was sewn into place we passed an electric current through the heart to stop it beating. We then made an incision into the left ventricle and used a cork bore instrument to remove a punched out circular piece of muscle to accommodate the Jarvik 2000 Heart. Inspection of this muscle under the microscope subsequently confirmed the very advanced state of deterioration causing Peter's heart failure.

Dr Jarvik in the mean time switched on the blood pump and tested it in a bowl of sterile salt solution. The sight of the fluid coursing through the pump is always a source of excitement. Jarvik passed the device to Frazier and myself and we carefully positioned it through the cuff and into the heart itself. The position was secured by tying two tapes in the cuff which slotted into a groove on the titanium shell. We then defibrillated the heart and allowed it to beat again and push out air from the system. We then joined the vascular graft from the Jarvik 2000 Heart to the graft already in place on the descending aorta. This fabric to fabric join needs very obsessional suturing and bleeds easily.

We then asked the Heart Lung Technician to throttle back on the bypass machine and allow some blood to stay in the heart. This allowed the heart to pump blood through the vascular graft and dispel air. Air in the circulation can damage the brain and other organs by blocking small blood vessels. When the de-airing process was complete we asked David Piggott to start ventilating the lungs again so that we could wean Peter from the heart lung machine and on to the Jarvik 2000 Heart. This was switched on at 10,000 r.p.m. and immediately began to convey blood away from the failing ventricle via the graft to the aorta and around the body. This completely changes the direction of blood flow to the brain and upper body because blood now enters the aorta just above where its passes from the chest to the abdomen. The other remarkable factor is that blood flow is continuous without a pulse. Physiologists had always considered that mammals needed a pulse in the circulation. Our experiments leading up to the Jarvik 2000 Heart Implants suggested otherwise but this was one of the first human experiences which confirmed that pulse is less important than anticipated.

Lack of pulse in the circulation complicates post-operative management of the patient which would normally depend on measurement of blood pressure and flow. In Peter's case we relied on new technology whereby a catheter continuously measures flow through the circulation independent of pulse. All other things that we could measure including pressure in the venous system, analysis of oxygen and carbon dioxide in the blood and kidney function all appeared satisfactory at this stage.

Clearly there was great excitement in the operating theatre and unbeknown to us at the time there was a spontaneous round of applause throughout the Lecture Theatre. Perhaps at this point we felt that our troubles were over and that Peter was safe. This was not to be the case. The most worrying problem was bleeding from all surgical sites because the blood would not clot. In addition the pressure in the artery to the lungs was too high as occurs in longstanding heart failure. David Piggott used nitric oxide gas to take the edge of this pressure. Frazier and myself then set about the task of stopping the bleeding. We had begun the operation at around mid-day and by 5.00pm we should have brought Peter back to the intensive care unit. In fact it took another two hours of stitching and coagulating small bleeding points before we were sufficiently confident to close the chest, turn Peter onto his back and leave the operating theatre. By this time Peter had received about 20 units of transfused blood. Finally we decided to insert the chest drains, close the chest and deliver Peter to Sister Desiree Robson in the Intensive Care Unit.

By this time it was 8.00pm and it proved difficult to obtain blood or clotting factors. We were forced to used clear fluid to replace blood loss and this worsened the coagulation problem. At 9.30pm after 2 litres of blood loss in the Intensive Care Unit we decided to return to the Operating Theatre, pack the chest and wait for clotting factors. Abnormal bleeding is a tedious problem in heart surgery. We put extra stitches in the oozing vascular graft but more stitches created more needle holes to bleed. Raw surfaces ooze blood and electrical coagulation just adds to the amount of damaged tissue. Eventually by 11.30pm we were satisfied that the bleeding was under control and again we left the Operating Theatre.

The inevitable consequence of low blood pressure and multiple blood transfusion is kidney failure. Sure enough within 12 hours we had trouble in maintaining urine flow. Peter's kidneys were poor before surgery and now it looked as if we would need dialysis. However the Jarvik Heart provided a circulation that Peter had not experienced for many years and before we needed to consider dialysis a brisk urine flow returned and everything began to improve. By measuring blood flow through the body we found that this beat with a pressure in the circulation of between 50 and 60 mm Hg. This is half that of a normal person with a pulse and was alien to the nurses and doctors looking after him. However all other parameters of organ function were entirely satisfactory and the pump output ranged between 6 and 8 litres with this pressure in the circulation.

Peter woke up the following morning but remained on the breathing machine for another 24 hours. By this time we were satisfied with his progress and confident of recovery. The whole team had remained by Peter's bedside during the first post-operative night but then Frazier had to return to Houston. His enormous experience with artificial hearts over the past 20 years had been invaluable in promoting Peter's survival. Rob Jarvik stayed for the next few days and was clearly delighted to see Peter resurrected by his invention. When Peter was weaned from the ventilator and Des Robson removed the tube from his lungs, his first words to us all were 'You Bastards'.

Stephen Westaby PhD FRCS MS
Consultant Cardiac Surgeon
July 2001

Glossary

Ace inhibitors   Angiotensin converting enzyme inhibitors – drugs used in the treatment of high blood pressure.

Analgesic   A drug used to control pain.

Angiotensin   A vasoconstrictor polypeptide hormone in the blood which acts to raise blood pressure.

Anti-Emetic   A drug used to control nausea and vomiting.

Beta-blockers   Drugs to lower blood pressure and help angina. They inhibit adrenaline and thus reduce heart rate.

Cardiomyopathy   A disease of the heart muscle resulting in poor circulation of blood into the aorta and arteries. The disease is progressive.

Catheter   A flexible plastic tube used to empty hollow organs, especially the urinary bladder, or to gain access to inaccessible parts of the body, especially the blood vessels and the heart. It acts as a drain.

Coronary artery disease   Sometimes known as arteriosclerosis. A blockage of the arteries to the heart that impedes the flow of blood to the heart muscle.

Digoxin   A heart drug that thins the blood, derived from the foxglove *digitalis*.

Diuretics   Water tablets. Drugs that increase the amount of water and salt in the urine. They are used to treat heart failure and high blood pressure.

Edema   Excessive accumulation of fluid, mainly water, in the tissue spaces of the body.

Endorphins   A group of morphine-like substances that are naturally produced in the body and for which morphine receptors exist in the brain.

Esophageal Cancer   Cancer of the esophagus, the gullet. This is a muscular tube linking the throat to the stomach. It is one of the cancers least responsive to treatment.

Enzyme inhibitors   Drugs used to inhibit the natural production of enzymes, which are biochemical catalysts that control the levels of chemical activity in the body.

Hypnotics   Sleeping tablets.

Inanition   A state of exhaustion or bodily disorder caused by inadequate nutrition.

Jarvik Pump   A Ventricular Assist Device (VAD). A small pump invented by Robert Jarvik that is placed in the lower left ventricle of the heart and pumps blood direct from there into the aorta thus assisting the heart's natural function.

Left ventricle   The lower chamber on the left of the heart, as opposed to the right ventricle on its right. The chamber receives oxygenated blood from the lung; the right ventricle sends blood in need of oxygenation to the lung.

Lipoma   A non-malignant tumour of fatty tissue. They can occur in fat anywhere in the body and grow slowly to form smooth, soft swellings. They seldom cause problems but can be removed if needed.

Lymph system   A system where tissue fluids are drained from the body through lymph vessels and returned via the blood to the veins.

Milrinone	A drug used to strengthen the heart function during heart failure or danger of failure.
Necrotic skin sores	These are round sores on the skin consisting of dead tissue. Essentially these show the same kind of decay that follows death.
Opioids	Naturally occurring peptides etc, in the body, that have an analgesic effect.
Opioid system	The system within the body that triggers the natural production of morphine-like substances to inhibit pain.
Opiate	Any pain-killing drug derived from opium.
Pain types	Pain can be understood in three ways according to source. These are nociopathic pain, neurological pain and ideopathic pain.
Palliation	Relief of severe suffering, either physical or mental, where such relief cannot be achieved by curative medicine.
Sedative	One of a group of drugs that include anti-anxiety drugs, sleeping drugs, anti psychotic drugs and some anti-depressants. See also Hypnotics above.
Thoracotomy	A surgical opening in the chest wall made to gain access to the interior. Most thoracotomies are made between the ribs in order to gain access to the heart. Sometimes a rib must also be removed to gain the access.
Vasodilators	Drugs that increase the blood flow in the veins by relaxing the vein walls, thus contributing to reduced blood pressure.

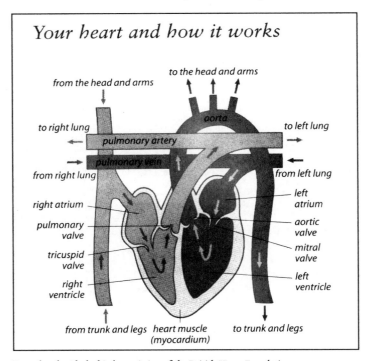

Your heart and how it works

Reproduced with the kind permission of the British Heart Foundation.

Index